To Gus

May your days in the woods
continue to be filled with
joy and fun.

With love from all at
the Secret Garden

4th August 2011

D1338675

HAMLYN

Birds' Eggs and Nests

A CONCISE GUIDE IN COLOUR

Birds' Eggs and Nests

by Jan Hanzák

Illustrated by

Přemysl Pospíšil and

Miroslav Rada

Hamlyn

London · New York · Sydney · Toronto

Translated by Margot Schierlová
Designed and produced by Artia for
THE HAMLYN PUBLISHING GROUP LIMITED
London • New York • Sydney • Toronto
Hamlyn House, Feltham, Middlesex, England
Copyright © Artia 1971
Reprinted 1973

ISBN 0 600 31241 0

Printed in Czechoslovakia

CONTENTS

INTRODUCTION

I should like, in introduction, to explain one or two questions related to the biology of birds with special reference to their nests and eggs which form the main subject of this book.

Birds differ in many respects from other vertebrates in their manner of reproduction. Like amphibians and reptiles, they lay eggs, but they do not then abandon them to their fate. They usually lay the eggs in a nest built by themselves and incubate them, keeping them warm with the heat of their own body until the young hatch out. They tend the eggs and the young and defend them against enemies. The young are not left to their own devices, like those of lower reptiles, but are trained or actually fed, both inside and outside the nest, for a long time, until they are capable of looking after themselves. As a rule, birds are model parents and their care of their offspring is generally so close to human standards that we sometimes tend to ascribe human properties to them. In fact, although birds possess considerable intelligence, their behaviour is controlled by instinct and not by reason.

BIRDS' EGGS

Formation, structure and appearance of the avian egg

All birds are oviparous, that is, they reproduce by laying eggs. There are no exceptions, as there are in the case of mammals, which are viviparous (bringing forth their young alive) but include some oviparous anomalies. Unlike the mammalian embryo, the avian embryo does not develop in the female's body but outside it after the egg has been laid. The egg is a product of the female organism, in which it is formed and acquires its final shape, structure and coloration. Despite the shortness of the route along which the egg passes through the female's body (from the ovary to the cloaca), it undergoes a number of changes on the way. Female birds have paired ovaries, but in most cases the right one is vestigial, so that only the left ovary and oviduct function. The ovary is shaped like a bunch of grapes and during the reproductory period it consists of a large number of follicles (vesicular ovarian follicles) in different stages of development. Only a few of the thousands of follicles in the ovary mature every year. The most mature and largest follicle bursts, releasing an ovum (egg cell), which migrates to the funnel-shaped mouth of the oviduct. The ovum is fertilized in the upper part of the oviduct before it starts to pass through it and before the egg membranes are formed. The oviduct is looped and in addition to a funnel-shaped mouth it has four sections lined with ciliated epithelium. This epithelium contains numerous glands, especially in the first part of the oviduct, where egg white (albumin) is formed round the ovum. This is the longest section of the oviduct. In the next part, the ovum, together with the albumin, is enclosed in a paper-like membrane. The third section of the oviduct secretes more, very thin, albumin, which penetrates through the membrane. Lastly, the walls of the egg secrete the shell, which gives the egg its ultimate shape. The fourth and most inferior part of the oviduct secretes only a given amount of mucus to enable the egg to be expelled through the cloaca. The egg is propelled through the oviduct by successive contractions (peristaltic movements) of the muscles of the oviduct walls. The egg membranes are formed very quickly — in the domestic fowl, for instance, the whole process takes only one day.

Having learnt something about the way in which the egg is formed, we can now go on to its internal structure. The main part of the avian egg is the yolk, together with the germinal disc. This is actually a single egg cell, the largest known in vertebrates (in large birds it may measure several centimetres). The yolk consists of two layers — white yolk (protoplasm) and yellow yolk (deutoplasm) — both of which form concentric layers. The protoplasm fills the centre of the yolk and extends as far as the germinal disc. During development, only the germinal disc undergoes cleavage, giving rise to the embryo; the rest of the yolk is simply nutrient material, which is gradually taken up by the embryo. The germinal disc is situated in the half of the ovum known as the animal pole, while the nutrient yolk is concentrated in the vegetal pole. The whole yolk is enclosed in a membrane known as the yolk sac.

The egg white consists of three layers. The outermost and least dense one is distributed below the shell membranes, the second one is dense and the innermost one, which is contiguous with the yolk sac, is again thin. The dense egg white contains

1. *Structure of bird's egg*
1 — *shell,* 2 — *outer layer of paper-like membrane,* 3 — *inner layer of paper-like membrane,* 4 — *air cell,* 5 — *chalazae (albumin cords),* 6 — *egg white,* 7 — *inner layer of thin egg white,* 8 — *yolk sac,* 9 — *white yolk,* 10 — *yellow yolk,* 11 — *eye*

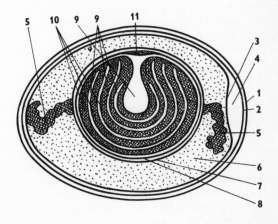

opalescent, spiral, dense albumin cords known as chalazae, which lead from the yolk to the shell membrane at either pole. They terminate freely in the egg white, however, thus buffering the yolk against mechanical shocks and helping it to keep its central position when the egg is turned. The animal pole of the ovum always comes to the top when the egg is turned, as the centre of gravity in the yolk is in the vegetal pole. The yolk and the albumin are enclosed in the colourless, transparent shell membrane consisting of two layers. At the blunt end of the ovum the layers are not contiguous and are separated by an air pocket, which increases in size during drying and incubation of the egg.

The whole of the egg is covered with a porous shell, composed mainly of calcium carbonate and trace amounts of salts and various organic substances. The number of pores is enormous. A hen's egg contains about 7,000 simple pores, while the pores in an Ostrich's egg are branched. The pores admit oxygen into the egg and allow removal of carbon dioxide formed during vital processes within the egg.

It is frequently stated that the blunt end of the egg always emerges first. It has been found, however, that in the domestic fowl the reverse occurred, and that in 84 % of cases the egg emerged pointed end first. There is no reason to doubt that the situation is any different in wild birds.

Birds' eggs have a wide range of colours. There are white eggs, plain-coloured eggs and eggs with differently coloured markings. Two pigments are mainly responsible for colouring — oocyan, a bile pigment derivative, and protoporphyrin, a blood pigment derivative. Oocyan is responsible for blue and green shades in basic coloration, while spots, and sometimes the general colour, are formed by protoporphyrin. Dispersed protoporphyrin is sometimes also found in pure white eggs.

In this book you will often come across the expressions 'surface' and 'deep' shell spots. If we look at spotted eggs we can see that some of the spots are on the surface and are more distinct, while others are actually in the shell and are less distinct. The first are the surface spots and the others the deep spots. Partial overlapping of these spots is quite common, indicating that the pigments are deposited successively during formation of the shell in the oviduct. Some species of birds lay eggs covered with a curious chalky coat, which may be spread over only part or all of the shell. This type of egg is found in Cormorants, pelicans, Gannets and Flamingos.

The colour of some birds' eggs changes during incubation. For example, the Great Crested Grebe lays pretty, bluish-white eggs. From contact with the rotting aquatic plants of which the nest is made, they gradually turn brownish, however. The light, bluish-green eggs of Herons also lose their pure, bright colour during incubation.

Besides their colouring, eggs are characterized by their shape, size, structure and the gloss of the shell, all of which must be taken into account when identifying them.

If a stone, fruit or vegetable is described as 'egg-shaped', we know what is meant. Any large collection of eggs, however, will show that this description is capable of a wide range of interpretation. In his book *Kein Ei gleicht dem anderen (No Two Eggs are Alike)*, Makatsch differentiates four basic shapes of birds' eggs — elliptical, oval, pointedly oval and pear-shaped — but as our illustrations show, there is a whole series of intermediate and extreme forms. In some groups of birds the shape of the egg is correlated with the shape of the female's pelvic girdle. As regards size, it is only logical that, among extant birds, the largest eggs are laid by the largest bird, the Ostrich, whose egg weighs 1,600 g (grams) and is equivalent in size to twenty hen's eggs. The smallest eggs are laid by humming-birds, whose huge tribe includes the smallest birds and the smallest eggs (0.25 g) in existence. It should be noted, however, that small birds, in relation to their size, lay larger eggs than the birds of big species. A Wren's egg is 13.7 % of the female's body weight, while in the Ostrich the proportion is only 1.7 %. It has not yet been discovered why some birds (the majority) lay dull eggs, while others lay beautiful, glossy eggs (woodpeckers, Rollers, Bee-eaters). The eggs of the South American tinamous have a very high gloss and one species actually lays black eggs. Although in most cases the coloration and markings of the eggs are species specific, in some cases they vary almost incredibly. Anyone who has seen a large collection of the eggs of the Black-headed Gull or of the Guillemot will have marvelled that such a thing is possible, as the eggs have different colours as well as markings.

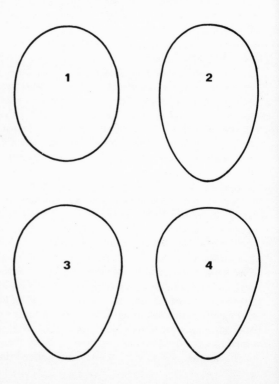

2. *Four basic shapes of birds' eggs*
1 — *elliptical,* 2 — *oval,* 3 — *pointedly oval,*
4 — *pear-shaped*

Another surprising finding is that closely related birds (like the Blackbird and the Song Thrush) have quite differently coloured eggs, while it can be difficult to distinguish between the eggs of the Collared Turtle-dove and the Pygmy Owl, which belong to entirely different and systematically remote orders, but lay very similar eggs.

The pigmentation of birds' eggs, like their plumage, shows different types of disguise. In species in which only the females sit on the eggs, especially in the case of ground-nesters, the females have good protective colouring. In order to make themselves still more invisible to their foes, they hide their nests in grass, among plants, or below the branches of shrubs. On leaving their nest, ducks cover their single-coloured eggs with down, with which the nest is abundantly lined, while grebes cover their light, single-coloured eggs with nest material. These measures are connected with heat regulation, as well as with protection, however. In general, it can be said that protective colouring of the eggs is not developed in species with no natural enemies, or which nest in large colonies where protection is assured by the whole nesting community. Hole-nesting birds likewise lay white or single-coloured eggs. Similarly, we do not find pronounced spotting of the eggs of many songbirds which conceal their nests very thoroughly. In the case of birds which nest in the open, however, such as the Nightjar, which lays its eggs on the bare ground, or a large number of waders (*Limicola*), which often build simple, more or less exposed nests, the eggs are coloured so as to blend perfectly with their surroundings. Anyone who has looked for the nest of the Little Ringed Plover (*Charadrius dubius*) in gravel alluvium from a river, or for the eggs of the Lapwing (*Vanellus vanellus*) in a meadow, will confirm that it is possible to wander about in the vicinity of the nest for hours without catching sight of the eggs. The above principles for protective colouring of the eggs are only very general: there are many exceptions and many cases which are hard to explain.

The number of eggs is fairly constant, not only for females of the same species, but often also for all species of the same systematic group. It depends primarily on mortality in the given species, on the number of natural enemies, and on the bird's mean life span. As a rule, species with many natural enemies, heavy losses and a short mean life span lay more eggs than species which live to a ripe old age. Birds with nidifugous young (leaving the nest soon after hatching) generally lay more eggs than birds with nidicolous young (which remain in the nest for some time). Guillemots *(Uria)* and some auks *(Alca)*, large seagulls and birds of prey lay only one egg. Two eggs are usually the rule for pigeons, humming-birds, cranes *(Grus)* and divers *(Colymbus)*. Waders lay three to four eggs. Gamebirds, swans, geese and ducks and some songbirds lay the most eggs. Clutches of over twenty eggs are rare (the Ostrich and the Partridge). In the case of species which, despite heavy losses, produce only small clutches, this deficiency is compensated by their nesting several times a year.

Annual egg production depends on the number of eggs in a clutch and on the annual nesting frequency. The environment is an important factor in this respect. Some birds nest more often and produce a greater average number of eggs in good years than in hungry years. For example, under favourable conditions the Great Tit will lay twenty-five to thirty eggs a year, while under adverse conditions the number falls, sometimes to only one third of this value. With some birds of prey and owls, the size of the clutch is also significantly correlated to the size of the small rodent population, especially in the case of birds living in the far north and dependent on the 'crop' of lemmings (the Snowy Owl and the Rough-legged Buzzard). The nesting period of the Barn Owl is considerably prolonged, and the number of young is much greater, in years with a prolific incidence of voles.

In most species of birds, loss of the eggs or young is followed in the female by renewed ovarian function, with resultant maturation of further follicles. The mating and nest-building instincts return and the bird lays a substitute clutch. If several clutches are lost, the bird may produce several substitute clutches, although not all birds are capable of replacing such losses. If eggs are removed during the laying period, it has the effect of making the bird continue laying. The females are in some way able to tell the number of eggs, either by sight or by touch, and to react automatically to a deficiency in their number. The domestic fowl and some ducks are classic examples of inducement to higher egg production. Continuous egg-laying is genetically stabilized in domestic fowls, so that they go on laying even when the eggs are not regularly removed, and it is not unusual for them to lay 300 eggs a year. The ability to continue laying if the eggs are regularly removed depends on the number of follicles. The Jackdaw, for instance, is capable of laying sixteen to thirty-five eggs and the female Magpie replenishes the clutch at such a rate that it sometimes dies of exhaustion. When replacing a lost clutch, birds usually use a new nest for the substitute clutch, as renewal of the function of the sex glands is also accompanied by renewal of the nest-building instinct. The smaller the clutch, the greater the certainty of replacement, is the general rule. The substitute clutch is usually smaller than the lost clutch.

There is no unequivocal answer to the question of the time of year for nest-building, as this depends primarily on the geographical position of the nesting place. In our own latitudes the seasons are very clearly defined and some preclude any possibility of breeding because of the temperature and lack of food. In the tropics, where conditions are more favourable, the situation is different, although even there certain rules apply.

In a given region, each species has its own limited, species specific nesting period, which is in accordance with the optimal requirements for the development and rearing of the young. Birds with a long incubation and rearing period start to nest sooner than those for which these periods are short. For example, the Bearded Vulture or Lammergeyer, which incubates its eggs for 56 days, begins to lay in January in Southern Europe and in September the young are still dependent on the parents. The same applies to several large birds of prey. In Central Europe, most small birds nest between April and June. Sedentary birds, which do not leave home during the winter, nest somewhat sooner, on average, than migratory birds. Late returners naturally nest much later as well.

Arctic birds have a very short nesting period, partly because most of them return late to their nesting place and partly because of the delayed appearance of spring. They have only a few weeks in which to nest and rear their young. Adaptation to these latitudes is manifested in the fact that the birds mate before returning to their nesting place, so that their gonads (sex glands) are already prepared. In Britain, which is influenced by the warm Gulf Stream, birds tend to nest sooner than in Central Europe and their nesting period is considerably longer. Some songbirds, such as the Wren, actually nest there during the winter.

The nesting period can be significantly influenced by the food supply. The Mediterranean Eleonora's Falcon *(Falco eleonorae)* probably lays its eggs at the beginning of August because at the time the young are reared the islands in this region swarm with huge flocks of migratory birds. The Crossbill chooses its nesting period to coincide with the time of maturation of conifer seeds. Its eggs and young can be found the whole year round, but most frequently from January to April, with the highest incidence in March. In tropical regions birds nest in the spring and summer, which correspond to our autumn and winter. The nesting period is influenced by the rainy season. The young of most species are hatched at the end of this season and are reared during the time of the greatest abundance of insects and fruit. Many species in tropical regions may nest the whole year round, however, especially where the dry and rainy seasons are not distinctly separated. Nevertheless, even here there is a tendency to nest during a given, limited time of the year. Some species may nest twice a year.

The Emperor Penguin of the Antarctic undergoes great deprivations while incubating its single egg. Like its cousin, the

King Penguin, it incubates the egg in a special fold of skin on its abdomen (in a kind of brood pouch). It prevents the egg from falling out by holding its legs tightly pressed together and remains like this through the long, dark July polar nights when the temperature sometimes falls to −50° C. The male and female take turns to incubate the egg, which they pass from one to the other by facing each other closely and rolling it over their feet. The parents tend their single, relatively small egg in this manner for 53 days and it also takes a long time before the young penguin attains independence. In March the following year the polar night returns with merciless regularity. This, at least, is one example of how, in exceptional cases, the incubation period may occur at an utterly unfavourable time of year.

Care of the eggs

Incubation of the eggs is instinctive behaviour stimulated during the nesting period. It is so automatic that many birds remain seated on the nest even if the eggs are removed. Some will even sit complacently on various dummies.

Apart from a few exceptions in which the eggs are left unguarded, one (or both) of the parents always sits on the eggs. As a rule, the male and female take turns at regular intervals. In some cases only the female incubates the eggs, but it is very rare for only the male to do so. We find almost regular alternation of the partners on the nest among divers, auks, seagulls, cranes, rails, pigeons, woodpeckers, starlings, warblers, etc. In some species they relieve each other at short intervals (sometimes after only a quarter of an hour), but usually after several hours. The Pratincole probably has 24-hour intervals, that is, the male one day, the female the next. Vultures change over after several days and penguins after 10—28 days. Alternation is not always regular and the male's share in incubation of the eggs is often smaller than that of the female.

A given degree of heat is necessary for successful development of the embryo. The source of this heat is the bird's body, which must thus be in close contact with the egg. The required incubation temperature is always slightly lower (39—40° C) than the bird's body temperature.

For better transfer of the heat of the bird's body to the eggs, bald patches known as brood spots are formed during the nesting period on the bird's belly. The feathers are either shed from these patches spontaneously, or are plucked out by the birds. The brood spots may be completely bald, or they may be thinly covered with down. The skin at these sites is highly vascularized, the blood capillaries are concentrated, forming a spongy tissue, and the fat is absorbed so as to do away with all possible obstacles to heat transfer between the bird's body and the eggs. Ducks have no brood spots, but during the nesting period the females acquire particularly fine down on their breast and belly (nest down), which they pack round the eggs, thus preventing the heat from escaping. Both males and females can have brood spots, according to which of them participates in incubation. Not infrequently both possess them.

It is known that birds usually lay their eggs in the early hours of the morning. Small species lay them at 24-hour intervals, so that the Chaffinch needs 5 days to lay a clutch of five eggs and the Great Tit 15 days for fifteen eggs. Larger species (of about the size of a pigeon) lay their eggs at 2-day intervals and the largest species at intervals of 3—4 days. The interval between the laying of the penultimate and the last egg is often longer than between the first eggs. In a few cases the female sits on the nest for some time before laying the first egg, but as a rule it does not 'go broody' until the first egg is laid. Hatching then follows almost exactly the same sequence as laying, thus sometimes giving rise to marked differences in the size of the young. Ducks, gamebirds and many other birds, on the other hand, do not start to incubate their eggs until the clutch is complete, so that the young are hatched within a very short period and are practically the same size. Some birds start to incubate their eggs shortly before the last one is laid.

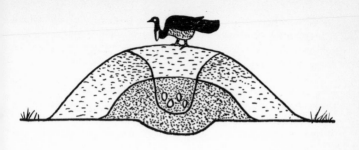

3. *Mound-builder on nest mound, in which the eggs are incubated by heat generated by rotting plant material*

We have already mentioned that not all birds sit on their eggs to incubate them. These form only a minute proportion of the total number of species, but they are so interesting that they deserve special attention. The mound-builders (Megapodides) live in the steamy forests of Australia and New Guinea. Unlike all other birds, they incubate their eggs in 'artificial incubators', in which there is no need for contact with the adult bird's body. The males of these species collect mould from the forest floor, containing leaves, different parts of plants, soil and sand, and form it into a mound in which the females lay their comparatively large eggs. When rain falls, the vegetable parts of the mound start to decay, producing considerable heat sufficient for successful development of the eggs. The temperature in the mound ranges from 29 to 36° C and is thus about 10 degrees higher than the environmental temperature. The female shows no further interest in the eggs, but the male remains near the mound, checks the temperature by touching it with some of the naked parts of its body (the under side of the wings, the head) and adds further material to the mound as required. In some species, several females lay their eggs in one mound. Other mound-builders utilize warm vulcanic springs or sun-heated sand for the incubation of their eggs, while sometimes a number

21

of factors are combined. After hatching out, the young remain several hours inside the 'incubator' and the male takes care to see that they are kept warm. The newly hatched young of mound-builders are the most advanced of all young birds. Their wings are fairly well developed and they are therefore capable of undertaking short flights very soon after leaving the egg. The young of the Brush Turkey *(Catheturus lathami)* can fly on the second day; they are completely independent and require no help from their parents.

The African Crocodile Plover *(Pluvianus aegyptiacus)* likewise makes use of the rays of the sun and the hot sand for the development of its two eggs. It buries them about 10 cm deep in the sand and sits over them only during the hottest part of the day to prevent them from becoming overheated.

It is not necessary for the clutches to be covered continuously by the adult birds. On occasion, the male and female leave the eggs unguarded for some time, if they need to find food or put their plumage in order. Cases are known in which they leave the nest for many hours without the development of the embryos being adversely affected. In principle, the eggs are more sensitive to temperature changes at the outset of incubation than towards the end. About six hours' absence of the parents from the nest need not have any effect, but if the nest is left unoccupied the whole night, the consequences are always disastrous. Violent shaking is far more injurious, however.

An important part of the care of the eggs is turning them over. Each time the parent returns to the nest, or otherwise at regular intervals, the sitting bird will lift the eggs and turn them over. Hens do this every half hour, even during the night. This must always be borne in mind when hatching eggs in an artificial incubator, as otherwise there will be high mortality among the embryos.

The time of incubation of the eggs is not necessarily related to the birds' size. For example, the Black Woodpecker and the tiny Chaffinch both sit on their eggs for 12—14 days. The time of incubation is more or less correlated to size only in the species of closely related groups. The Raven sits on its eggs 21—23 days, the Carrion Crow 18—20 days and the Jay only 11—13 days. The time needed for incubation of the eggs of songbirds is 12—18 days, for pigeons an average of 17 days, for game-birds 21 days and for eagles 34—38 days. On evaluating the various species and systematic groups, we find some correlation between the time of incubation and the degree of security during the breeding period. Species with inaccessible nesting sites (and therefore with greater security) usually sit on their eggs longer than species exposed to frequent danger. Auks, Gannets, petrels, shearwaters and albatrosses incubate their eggs for relatively long periods and some of the species of these groups, with incubation periods of up to 60 days, are among the record holders in this respect.

Care of the young

Young birds are hatched without any assistance. Success depends on good development and physical fitness. The shell is not easy to break and it is punctured, usually at the blunt end, by a special implement — the egg tooth. This is a horny protuberance formed at the tip of the embryo's upper mandible and is lost a few days after hatching. Only woodpeckers and their allies also have an egg tooth on the lower mandible.

As soon as the egg tooth punctures the shell, which has grown thin by the end of incubation, the young bird presses on the fragile obstacle with its head, legs and wings until it cracks and, piece by piece, drops away. Complete liberation takes several hours to 2 days. Young grebes are hatched exceptionally quickly, sometimes in only a few minutes. It is believed that this is a form of adaptation to the dangers of their watery environment, as the young bird would be in danger of suffocation if water entered the egg. In species with nidifugous young, the shells are generally left in or round the nest, while in other species the parents quickly either remove or eat them. Uncovered, strikingly marked eggs with a light inner surface might draw the attention of foes to the presence of desirable prey (the newly hatched young). The weight of eggs decreases during incubation. We all know that unfertilized eggs, if placed in water, sink to the bottom, while fertilized and incubated eggs float. A newly hatched young bird weighs on an average only two thirds of the weight of the fresh egg.

The stage of development of newly hatched young varies. In general we can differentiate two groups: nidifugous young and nidicolous young. There are many intermediate groups, but we know by now that it is not always possible to express an unequivocal opinion when evaluating many phenomena in the nest biology of birds. We likewise cannot decide which of these two groups is the original one, as the criteria do not always give us a clear answer. Perhaps only the fact that reptiles, which are the birds' closest relatives, are nidifugous, while the most highly organized birds — songbirds — are nidicolous warrants the assumption that the nidifugous type is the more primitive.

Cursorial birds, fowl-like birds, bustards, rails and ducks — all of which live and nest mainly on the ground or on water — can be regarded as examples of nidifugous birds. Their young leave the nest from within a few hours to 2—3 days after hatching and are largely independent. They are covered with fine down, are capable of active movement from a very early age and, in the case of aquatic birds, are able to swim well. They either find their food themselves, or are given it or guided to it by the parents. In a short time they learn what is good to eat and what is not. The adult birds train them for a long time, show them where to find sources of food, warn them of dangers and defend them against enemies. During cold weather and at night the young instinctively seek shelter beneath the parents' wings and plumage. In the case of species living on water, there is danger of the young birds' downy coat becoming wet. Swans and grebes carry their young in the feathers under their wings and on their back while swimming and grebes actually dive with them. Oil is transferred from the parents' plumage to the downy coat of the young, so that they can remain in the water for a comparatively long time. If we encounter a family of nidifugous birds, the young instantly scatter and go into hiding. The females of some species try to draw intruders away by pretending to be injured or by assuming threatening behaviour. Among our own birds which belong to this group we find species which nest above the ground, such as the Golden-eye, which nests high up in tree hollows or in artificial nesting-boxes. The young are thus obliged to climb up the sides of the hollow to the opening by means of their sharp claws' and to jump to the ground, often from a height of many yards. This acrobatic performance does not usually have serious consequences. As already mentioned, we have an extreme example of nidifugous birds in the mound-builders, whose young leave the nest mound and make their first attempts to fly soon after hatching and are entirely independent of their parents.

At the opposite pole we find nidicolous birds, which form the majority. The newly hatched young of these birds are quite helpless, blind and naked or covered only with fine down. They are completely dependent on their parents, which feed them

4. *Difference between nidicolous young (left) and non-nidicolous young (right) of same age*

assiduously for as long as they are confined to the nest and often after they are able to leave it. These young have a curiously formed and strikingly coloured gullet. Its shape, and the movements of the young bird's head, act as a feeding stimulus to the adult birds and show them the target. The gullet of the young of some songbirds actually contains luminous light-reflecting tubercles.

The begging movements of the young are purely reflex in character and are immediately activated by changes in the intensity of the surrounding light if a shadow falls on the nest, or by the sound of their parents' voices. The feeding of the young by the adult birds is likewise an automatic reaction, which can also be induced artificially by showing them dummy reproductions of the gullet of their young. The young birds consume a large amount of food and keep the parents constantly busy. As a result, they grow very rapidly. Within 14 days the young of songbirds catch up in weight with the young of nidifugous birds of the same size and soon afterwards outstrip them. While feeding their young, the adult birds lose some of their timidity.

Information on the performance of some species of birds during the feeding period is provided by actographs — instruments which automatically record the number of journeys made by the birds to their nest. Coal-tits and Nuthatches bring food to the nest 350—550 times a day (and even oftener towards the end of the nesting period), sparrows 150—250 times, the Common Redstart 250—400 times and the Great Tit, just before the young are fledged, up to 800 times.

Nidicoles primarily include songbirds and most of the following: pelicans and their allies, birds of prey, owls, pigeons, woodpeckers and rollers, i.e. birds which, generally speaking, nest high above the ground, mainly in trees. The two groups also differ in other respects, though not always completely. Nidifugous birds generally lay larger eggs with a richer yolk, evidently because the embryos require better nutrition, as the newly hatched young are sensorily more advanced than those

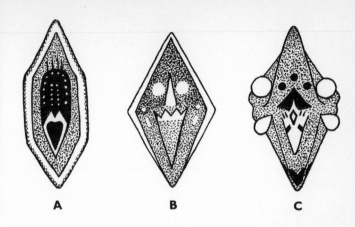

A   B   C

5. *View of inside of beak of young of some nidicolous birds*
A — *Bearded Tit*, B — *Cuckoo*, C — *Ribbon Weaver-finch with fluorescent papillae on edge of beak*

of nidicolous birds. Comparison of the size of the clutches in the two groups will show that those of nidicolous birds are, on an average, smaller, but this deficiency is compensated by there being several breeding periods a year. Conversely, nidifugous birds have large families, but nest only once a year. This is evidently due to lack of time, as nidifugous species care for their young much longer than nidicolous birds. If a second clutch were laid, there would not be sufficient time to complete the rearing of the young. The families of nidifugous birds generally remain united a very long time.

Some birds, such as auks, gulls and terns, are born with a downy coat, but remain in the nest for a long time and are fed by the parents, sometimes even after they have left the nest. These birds form a link between the two main groups.

The young are fed in a diversity of ways. Some birds only place food in front of their young, while others regurgitate it

27

from their crop on to the nest or directly into the young bird's beak. Some give the food to their offspring whole, while others pre-digest it or divide it into fragments. Nidifugous birds, whose young soon fend for themselves, have the fewest worries. Everybody has doubtless observed how busily chickens hunt for food when only a few days old.

The family relationship between the adult and young birds may persist long after the latter have left the nest. With geese, swans, cranes and some birds of prey, the family is still intact the following spring. The families of small birds soon break up: the adult birds start to nest again or part company with their offspring.

Brood parasitism

Birds which do not rear their young themselves but entrust their eggs and the care of their young to other birds, form a special group. This phenomenon, known as brood parasitism, is found among some weavers, icterids, honey-guides, cuckoos and even ducks. Different degrees of brood parasitism are found among tropical cuckoos. Some build their own nests and lay single-coloured eggs, while others place several eggs in the nest of another species, but the young do not throw out the foster parents' young as those of our own Cuckoo do.

Brood parasitism attains the highest degree in the Cuckoo, in which it has been thoroughly studied. The female Cuckoo lays twelve to twenty eggs, and sometimes more, during a single season. The eggs are small in proportion to the size of the bird, but because of the thickness of their shell they are always heavier than those of the foster parents. At present, about 100 foster parent species are known, but only some of them can be described as regular hosts of Cuckoo eggs. Few birds' eggs are so variably coloured as Cuckoo's eggs, which are coloured and marked so as to correspond as closely as possible to those of their different insectivorous hosts. We have already mentioned that non-parasitic cuckoos have single-coloured eggs. The Cuckoo can also produce plainly coloured eggs, which it places in the nests of birds which lay single-coloured eggs. This means that different biological races, with eggs corresponding in colour to those of the host species, have developed among Cuckoos during phylogenesis.

The mimicry of Cuckoos' eggs developed selectively over innumerable generations. The host birds simply threw out eggs dissimilar to their own, resulting in their destruction and hence in the gradual disappearance of Cuckoos accustomed to lay their eggs in the nests of unsuitable hosts. The reverse process occurred where the parasite egg resembled the eggs of the host bird. In this case, the young Cuckoos prospered, the habit of laying eggs in the nests of a suitable species became genetically fixed and a biological race of Cuckoos whose eggs conformed to those of the host bird gradually developed, thus assuring its further existence. Cuckoos' eggs have an exceptionally thick shell and are not easily broken if the Cuckoo places it carelessly, or lays it hurriedly, in the foreign nest. When laying an egg in a nest from which the host bird is absent, the Cuckoo usually removes one or two of the original eggs, frequently swallowing them. Another form of adaptation is shortening of the time of embryogenesis. Cuckoos' eggs mature in $12\frac{1}{2}$ days Cuckoos therefore generally lay their eggs when the host bird starts to lay, so that the young Cuckoo hatches out sooner than the young of the foster parents, or at the same time. Acting on a special instinct, the young Cuckoo makes sure that it is the only young bird in the nest and that there are no other competitors for food in the form of foster siblings. The naked back of the young Cuckoo is particularly sensitive to touch and any objects in the nest with which it comes into contact, whether eggs or young, are thrown overboard. It tries to hold the object on its back, supporting itself by its still undeveloped wings, legs and beak, until its back is on a level with the edge of the nest, where the egg or young bird is dropped over. The young Cuckoo thus becomes the only centre of interest of its foster parents, which feed it as assiduously as if it were their own. It consumes as much food as five to six young songbirds and doubles its weight in 3 days. The foster parents keep the intruder fed for 5 weeks, until it is much larger than they are.

6. *Young cuckoo throwing host's eggs out of nest*

BIRDS' NESTS

Building material and construction

Many groups of animals build nests for their eggs or offspring. Examples are even to be found among invertebrates. Among the vertebrates, nest-building is a common phenomenon in amphibians, reptiles, fishes and mammals, but this instinctive behaviour is most highly developed in birds, which include some of the best builders in the animal kingdom. The laying of eggs in nests is a characteristic feature of avian biology. Nest-building is not only of practical significance for incubating the eggs and rearing the young, but also plays an important part in the social life of birds, during wooing and mating. In many cases, the completed or partly completed nest is a bait for the unpaired female and is an important factor in mating in general. It provides shelter for the eggs, protects the sitting bird against danger and bad weather and is a temporary refuge for the young, especially in the case of nidicolous birds, whose young are confined to the nest for a considerable length of time. Nest-building is associated in birds with development of the sex glands and is typical instinctive behaviour.

The nest is usually made of different parts of plants, which nature offers in abundance. These are primarily branches and twigs collected on the ground near the nest and corresponding in size to the size of the builder. Large birds sometimes break them off directly in the tree-tops. Many birds employ blades of grass and reeds as well as twigs. With most birds, the dry parts of plants — blades, stems, leaves, rootlets, bast and bark — are popular as a building material. The finest materials employed include moss, lichens, the hairy parts of plant seeds and plant fluff, which, like materials of animal origin, such as feathers, hairs, wool and cobwebs, are generally used for lining the nest. Large birds which make their nests of branches and twigs often reinforce them with soil and turf, so that they are heavy as well as strong. Soil is used by the Song Thrush, which smears the inner walls of the nest with a mixture of soil and wood mould, and it forms the main raw material for the nest of many other birds. The Nuthatch uses soil to narrow the entrance to its nest-hole, but it is only a primitive mason compared with swallows, martins or the Rock Nuthatch, whose entire nest is composed of small lumps of mud stuck together and reinforced with vegetable material. These nests may be open from above, or closed, with a simple opening or a long passage for an entrance (the Rock Nuthatch) and are made of damp soil and clay. You will no doubt recall having seen groups of swallows and martins busily collecting these materials round the edge of pools of water in the spring. Some species of American ovenbirds build large spherical or hemispherical clay nests on thick branches. The walls are 2.5—4 cm thick and are divided inside into several compartments. An ovenbird's nest weighs up to 4.5 kg, while the builder weighs only 78 g. Swifts reinforce their nests with saliva, which solidifies on contact with the air. Our own Swift uses blades of grass and cereals, hairs and feathers, stuck together with saliva, as its main building material. The thin-walled nest of the Asian Edible-nest Swiftlet is made entirely of solidified saliva and is attached to the rocky walls of caves. The natives collect these nests, which they regard as a great delicacy. The Palm Swift, or Klecho, builds a tiny nest (in relation to its size) for its single egg and attaches it to a branch of a tree. The nest is a thin shell made of fragments of bark, lichen and hard parts of plants, stuck together with saliva.

Nest-building techniques are inherited. It would be impossible for a Swallow to build its nest in a tree, like the Chaffinch, or for the Chaffinch to make a clay nest like the Swallow's. The Sky Lark always nests on the ground and the Oriole in the tree-tops. Nevertheless, circumstances sometimes compel birds to depart from their usual habits. We may find the Tawny Owl nesting on the ground, if there is a deficiency of natural hollows, while in flooded areas Mallards will often nest in hollow trees or the old nests of other, tree-nesting, birds. Geographical position is also an important factor in this respect. In Central Europe falcons nest on rocks, in Northern Europe and Siberia on trees, and in the tundra on the ground. Similarly, in Europe the Osprey builds its nest in trees, but in North America it also nests on the ground. This adaptability in the choice of a nesting site is sometimes manifested over a very small area and is difficult to explain. Night Herons, round a single pond, always nest in the tree-tops, but from time to time, in the same place, a large part of the colony will nest among the rushes. The same applies to the Heron.

Is the nest built by the male or the female? There is no one answer to this question, as observations often differ within individual orders and families. In polygamous species, it is usual for the female to build the nest, but this also applies to most monogamous species; the male's duties consist rather in vocal demarcation and defence of its domain. Even in species in which both partners participate in the building of the nest, the male's role is often confined simply to fetching the material for the nest, or to accompanying the female on the same errand, while the actual building is done by the female. In frigate-birds the position is reversed and it is the female which fetches the material, while the male actually builds the nest. In some cases only the work of building the rough foundations is shared, while the female is responsible for the internal fixtures and the lining. Among some waders, the male hollows out the inside of the nest, by scraping or turning it, and the female fetches the modest lining which consists of parts of plants found in the immediate vicinity. Even when both partners fetch the material for the nest, most of the work usually devolves on the female.

It is rare for the male to be the chief constructor. Among woodpeckers, however, it is mainly the male which is responsible for hollowing out the nest hole. In species in which coloration dimorphism is reversed, that is, in which the female is brightly coloured and the male plainly coloured (the Painted Snipe, phalaropes), the male is responsible for rearing the young as well as for building the nest. Males without a partner sometimes build several nest foundations, thereby tempting a female to join them. After pairing, the female chooses one of these foundations and completes the nest. This phenomenon is familiar among Herons, for example. The males of other species actually build virtually complete nests, in which only the lining is missing. They then leave the choice and completion of the nest to the female. The nests not used for breeding (play nests) are employed only by the male (cock nests), or for the young to sleep in (sleeping nests). The best known bird of this type is the Wren, which builds indefatigably all over its domain. The community nests of the weaver *Ploceus philippinus* are also built entirely by the males. As soon as they have acquired a female, the males start to build a second, or even a third, nest and look round for further mates.

Comparison of the data of various authors on the part played by the male and female in building the nest, will reveal a number of discrepancies. This may be due to incomplete and inexact observation, but also to differences in the behaviour of individuals of the same species. Knowledge of the nest biology of birds has quite a number of weak points in this respect and we would need to supplement or verify the data on many common species.

The time required for building the nest can be influenced by a variety of factors, such as the supply of building materials, the weather, the season, the size of the nest and the amount of work done by each partner. Small birds usually build their nests in 4—6 days. The complicated spherical nest of the Penduline Tit requires 3—6 weeks' work by both partners. The Golden Eagle builds its great nest for two whole months and the Osprey needs about 14 days. Migratory birds which return to their nesting site later than other individuals of the same species build their nests more quickly. For example, Night Herons which arrive at the beginning of April build their nests in 8—9 days, while later couples returning in May not only build a simple nest in 7 days, but also manage to lay three eggs during this period. The Edible-nest Swiftlet takes from 33 to 41 days to make its nest. Birds build their nests most actively during the morning and early evening.

The nesting instinct is not suppressed after the eggs have been laid. On the contrary, it is often manifested during the breeding period and even while the young are being reared. In many species, the addition of fresh parts to the nest has been observed during these periods. As a rule, however, only the edges of the nest are raised, so as to make it deeper inside and thus prevent the eggs or young from falling overboard. Some species which nest near water (waders, ducks) increase the height of their nests if the water level rises (as after heavy rain). If the water rises suddenly, however, most of the nests are lost in any case.

It is a popular fallacy that a bird's nest is a kind of home, to which the birds always return, if only to sleep, even after the breeding season is over, and that they use the same nest for breeding several times in succession. As a rule, after leaving the parental nest, the young never return. Exposed nests are also seldom used for egg-laying more than once. Songbirds in particular regularly leave their old nests and build new ones, even if the clutch is lost. Such birds often pull the old nest to pieces and build a new nest from the fragments. In the case of large birds, which build correspondingly large nests, the situation is different. Storks return to their laboriously built nests every year and repair and improve them. In this way the nest may last for years and weigh up to two tons.

Some large birds of prey have several nests scattered over their domain, which they use in succession. Small, hole-nesting songbirds also show considerable predilection for the same nest, which they will defend stubbornly against their own kind or birds of other species. The number of birds which return to their nest to sleep is exceedingly small. The majority prefer to spend the night in trees and bushes, or in the grass. Swallows and starlings have their favourite common sleeping quarters among reeds, while crows sleep in copses, to which they return to sleep in company every year from great distances. Swallows sleep among rushes, but their cousins, the martins, fly back in the evening to their clay nests below the eaves. Even individuals of the same species may have different sleeping habits. Some sparrows will flock to special trees to sleep, while others will return to their own untidy nests.

A very few species of birds do not build a nest at all, but lay their eggs either on the bare ground or on some other surface. These include the Nightjar, the Barn Owl, the Eagle Owl, auks and some species of penguins. Some species of woodpeckers and owls and the Hoopoe lay their eggs on the floor of tree-holes without providing them with a special underlay. Many birds in which the building instinct is not developed lay their eggs in the nests of other species, or even in mammals' dens and burrows. Some birds of prey, such as the Kestrel, the Lesser Kestrel and the Hobby, often use nests abandoned by crows. The Green Sandpiper, whose cousins nest on the ground, lays its eggs in old thrush nests.

The simplest nest is a plain, unlined hollow formed by the bird in mud, sand or soil, as in the case of some gulls, terns and waders. Some species of these orders line the hollow with a thin layer of different parts of plants, however. In the colonies of one species of tern we find some nests without a lining, while in further nests the eggs are surrounded by a small rampart of blades of grass, in others they rest on a deep layer of vegetable material and other nests again have a shallow basin. We can see from this example that development of the building instinct can vary within the same species. The most efficient ground-nesters line their nests with grass or twigs.

Nesting sites

Ground-nesting is evidently the most primitive form. This group of birds obviously includes the flightless birds like Ostriches and penguins, and of the others we should at least mention game-birds, swans, geese and ducks, rails, waders and, among the songbirds, some wagtails and buntings. Within these groups we always find species which differ in some way from the majority, however. Most ground-nesters build well-constructed, tidy, and sometimes intricate nests, which in addition to rough foundations have a well lined with fine material (in ducks fine down plucked by the female from its own belly). In this group we also find covered nests (warblers) and clay nests (Flamingos).

Rock-nesting is a special form of ground-nesting and occurs mainly among birds which live in colonies on steep or shelving rocks and on islands. We must be careful in our differentiation, however, as some birds which nest on cliffs belong to the group of hole- and niche-nesters. Ground-nesters also include the mound-builders, whose curious nests have already been described above.

Some aquatic birds nest on the ground near the water, others at a distance (ducks, divers), while others build their nests in the shallows, surrounded by water (geese, swans, coots). A small minority of aquatic birds build floating nests, which are naturally usually concealed in clumps of aquatic plants and seldom float on the open water. This type of nest is built by grebes. The concealment and camouflage of the nests and eggs of birds nesting on the ground or on water varies. Some of these birds nest right in the open, in sand and mud without any vegetation (terns, some waders), while others build their nests in short grass (the Lapwing). Most species, however, are led by instinct to hide their nests from their enemies in tangled vegetation, under bushes, in clumps of couch grass and sedge or under tufts of grass. The urge to ensure the greatest possible safety for the eggs is in some species so strong that on leaving the nest, the bird either covers them with the down used for lining the

7. *Two types of weaver birds' nests.*
On left: Vieillot's Black Weaver (Ploceus nigerrimus), on right:
Baya Weaver (Ploceus philippinus)

nest (ducks) or with the material used in its construction (grebes). Some ground-nesters display a tendency to niche-nesting, while others protect their eggs by building spherical, covered-in nests.

Understandably, birds, being capable of active flight in the air, also make considerable use of high building sites, where their nests are safer. Trees, bushes and tall plants are therefore the commonest sites for birds' nests. Like ground-nesters, some birds of this group simply lay their eggs on a few twigs carelessly placed across a forking branch (some pigeons). Others — the majority — build neat nests in a trough in a branch, in the tree-tops, on thick branches or on the thin twigs right at their tip. In this group we also include species which weave a nest in tangled undergrowth close to the ground, or suspend it from blades of grass or reeds. Some of these birds display exceptional skill as builders. The Reed Warbler must possess vast experience as a constructor to be able to hang its basket-like nest so in-geniously between reeds. And what about the spherical, en-closed nest of the Roller, tucked away out of sight on the trunk of a tree? The best builder among our own birds is undoubtedly the Penduline Tit, which makes a pouch-like nest woven together out of fine material and suspends it from the thinnest twigs at the end of branches of trees and bushes, usually high above water. It is surpassed in this art only by some tropical weavers, which make intricately woven nests with long, tubular entrances, or complex nests housing whole colonies. We find many master-builders among tropical birds, such as the icterids and sunbirds. When constructing their nests, some species plait loops by which to attach the nest firmly to twigs and stems.

Nests built in the open and not influenced by the walls of some cavity can be shaped and held in position in varying ways. Basket type nests are held fast by their rim in a forked branch. Basin type nests are usually deep and are placed in the fork between trunk and branch, in slanting forks in the branches or in grass and other plants, or are suspended from blades of grass, etc. The extremely shallow nests of the Ring Dove and Gold-

8. *Red-billed Quelea making loop during building of nest*

crest, on the other hand, lie unsupported directly on a branch. The first transition to enclosed nests is exemplified in those surmounted by an imperfectly woven roof. Titmice, and sometimes sparrows, Wrens and Penduline Tits, make typical spherical nests, in some species with a tubular entrance. We have already mentioned the diversely constructed and complicated nests of weavers. The Tailor-bird of South Africa makes a container for its nest by folding a leaf cornet-wise and literally sewing the edges together with plant fibres.

Hole-nesting is by far the safest method and is very widespread among birds. Here again there are different forms of development. Some species content themselves with a mere trace of a hole and build in a hollow in a rotting tree stump or in the cavity left by a broken branch, behind loose bark, in an opening or crack in sandy or clay walls or in a heap of stones, so that the nest is not covered in on all sides. Other species nest in deep cavities in rotting trees or in deep underground burrows.

Hole-nesting is so highly developed in woodpeckers, barbets and some tits that they often hack out roomy nest-holes themselves in healthy wood (woodpeckers) or rotting wood. Birds which nest in holes in trees or in burrows are known as hole-nesters, as distinct from niche-nesters, which nest in hollows.

Very often there is a serious deficiency of suitable holes, especially where natural conditions have been altered by man. As a result, woodpecker holes are frequently used by other birds unable to make a hole for themselves. For example, Stock Doves, Rollers, different species of owls and starlings often nest in woodpecker holes. The Nuthatch adapts these holes to its small size by walling in and narrowing the entrance. Some tropical hornbills behave in a similar manner. The male walls the female in during the breeding period, often until the young are fledged, leaving only a small aperture through which to pass food.

Many birds nest in the ground or in sandy or clay walls, in holes which they find or excavate themselves. We find a whole series of examples of this type of nest among songbirds (Mynahs, Sand Martins) and other orders (kingfishers, bee-eaters, some auks and parrots). Even the burrows of mammals may be utilized. For instance, the Western Burrowing Owl makes a grass-lined nest in rabbit burrows, sometimes up to 3 m underground. The Ruddy Shelduck requires a larger burrow, while our own Coal-Tit will sometimes make do with an empty mouse-hole. In exceptional cases, birds nesting in tree-holes may also nest on the ground (the Stock Dove, the Roller). We can see from pigeons that the way of nesting may vary considerably within related groups. The Stock Dove nests in holes, while the Ring Dove and the Turtle Dove build shallow, dish-like twig nests. Since pigeons' eggs are white, we assume that hole-nesting is the older form in this group. We likewise conclude that in the case of birds which build large nests in tree-holes, this form of nesting developed secondarily, while in species which hack out a hole themselves and lay their eggs on the unpadded floor of the cavity it is the primary form. We can help many hole- and niche-nesters by providing them with artificial nesting-boxes, to which they take very quickly and which they often use in preference to natural holes.

Some birds actually nest in dark caves. Some nightjars, Oilbirds and Edible-nest Swiftlets are typical inhabitants of underground caverns, and Rock Doves and young Jackdaws also nest there.

In some species the nesting instinct has been extinguished: they either acquire a nest by fighting for it, or use old, abandoned nests. This is a very widespread phenomenon. To come close to home, the Long-eared Owl likes to nest in empty crows' nests. The use of woodpecker holes is also regarded as nest appropriation, and so is the use of anthills, termite mounds and mammals' burrows. Some species employ foreign nests on principle, while in others, some couples build their own nest and the rest prefer foreign nests. It is difficult to say why this is so. It is not uncommon for two females of the same or different species to lay their eggs in one nest. Even three have been known to employ the same nest. As an example there are the exceedingly large clutches of some herons and ducks, which indubitably come from two or three females of the same species. In ducks and certain other birds, cases have been recorded in which two females of different species laid their eggs in the same nest. For the sake of consistency, we must also consider habitation of the lower 'storey' of the nests of large birds (birds of prey, herons, storks) by some small birds as nest appropriation. In Europe, Starlings and both our species of sparrows in particular are included among these 'subtenants'. This phenomenon is naturally also found elsewhere. For instance, the Grey-breasted Parrakeet of South America likes to nest in the nests of large birds of prey. However, cases in which the nest is actually shared, such as finding a thrush and a Dunnock side by side in a thrush's nest, are very rare.

Colony nesting

Another striking and widespread phenomenon in the nest biology of birds is the formation of nesting colonies. The size of the colony may vary from a few couples to a large number. The main reason why birds collect in colonies during the breeding season is evidently that there is safety in numbers and that the eggs and young can be protected more effectively against bird and mammal foes. Few birds or beasts of prey will venture into a screeching flock of parent birds all attacking at once. Another factor in colony formation is an abundant food supply near the colony, or the isolated character of the nesting site and the absence of any other nesting facilities in the neighbourhood.

The nesting territory, which is so strongly developed in most birds, is also present in birds which nest in colonies, but their domain is confined to the area immediately round the nest. Different degrees of the colony-nesting impulse are found in birds. Some species generally nest individually and combine to form colonies only in given circumstances. For example the Great Crested Grebe, whose couples usually nest separately, will on occasion form small groups of nests. In some regions a given species will nest individually, while in others it regularly forms nesting colonies. Again we have an example in the Great Crested Grebe which shows a greater tendency to colony-nesting the further east it is found. Conversely, some birds which normally nest in colonies may here and there build solitary nests, such as the Heron and other species of herons, or other typical colony-nesters like the Rook. In the case of the White Stork, the reverse applies. This bird builds solitary nests in Central Europe, but in regions where there is an abundance of water there is a stork's nest on practically every roof in the villages, and sometimes several nests on one building or one tree.

Although small groups of nests can also be considered as colonies, the most arresting are those in which the number of nesting couples can be counted in hundreds or thousands. These huge colonies are typical chiefly of birds living near water and of marine birds, although they are by no means uncommon even among songbirds (crows, some swallows, the Rose-coloured Starling, weavers). The reports of nineteenth-century ornithologists speak of heron, ibis, Spoonbill and cormorant colonies thousands strong in the thickets and rushes round river creeks in the Balkans. This is simultaneously an example of mixed colonies, with several species of birds living in company. Flamingos form large colonies beside brackish water, while huge colonies of pelicans, Gannets, Fulmars, penguins, auks, gulls and terns sometimes enliven cliffs, seashores and lonely islands. It is amazing how many birds will often congregate to nest in a small space. The Emperor Penguin used to form colonies numbering a million individuals on the islands to the south of New Zealand. The largest breeding colonies include those of the Great Shearwater *(Puffinus gravis)* on two islands of the Tristan da Cunha group in the South Atlantic, one of which comprises 300,000 birds and the other is said to number about 4,000,000.

Mixed colonies are often found on cliffs or on rocky islands in the sea, where hundreds of couples of several species of auks, Razorbills and Puffins may live close together, side by side, with Kittiwakes, shearwaters and other species. Unfortunately, indiscriminate plundering by human beings in the past has in many cases severely reduced the size of these colonies, and even today the fate of a number of famous colonies is still in the balance. Man's destructive activities have a disastrous effect on colony-breeding birds, as whole colonies can be wiped out in a relatively short time. Indeed, some species have been killed off altogether, such as the flightless Great Auk, which once lived on the islands round Iceland, and the Passenger Pigeon in the forests of North America.

Some species of birds of prey which do not build a nest find welcome accomodation in colonies of tree-nesting birds and it is almost a general rule for large colonies of herons or crows to have as their guests one or two couples of birds of prey, which usually keep the peace with them. The Falcon, the Saker Falcon and the Black Kite and other birds of prey, according to the circumstances, are frequent co-inhabitants in heron colonies. However, crows and Ravens nesting inside or at the edge of colonies generally seize every opportunity to steal eggs and young birds.

Nesting territories

For a couple of a given species of bird to be able to breed successfully and in peace and to feed and rear their young without difficulty, they must have the freedom of a certain area round the nest, which they regard as their territory. This hypothetical domain has fixed limits which the birds maintain and defend against other individuals of the same species. Competition is particularly pronounced in species which are very plentiful in a given habitat and whose territories are crowded together in close contact. The nest plays an important role, since the nesting territory is determined, as a rule, by the position of the nest, which generally lies in the centre. As a result, various couples of the same species will divide up a habitat between them, and since each territory must have a minimum area, natural regulation of the number of nesting couples ensues. The size of the nesting territory varies with the species and is primarily dependent on food requirements. Birds which live on a specialized diet, such as birds of prey, have to fly long distances in search of food. They therefore have a larger radius than insectivorous birds which find sufficient food for the whole of their large family over a small area round the nest. Let us have a look at the size of some birds' territories which are given below in square metres:

Golden Eagle	93,000,000 sq m
Mistle Thrush	500,000 sq m
Song Thrush	40,000 sq m
Robin	6,000 sq m
Chaffinch	4,000 sq m

Coot	4,000 sq m
Willow Warbler	1,500 sq m
Blackbird	1,200 sq m
King Penguin	0.5 sq m
Black-headed Gull	0.3 sq m

The size and shape of the area depends on the configuration of the terrain and the character of the vegetation. The nesting territory of the Great Crested Grebe is oval, as this bird primarily defends the area round the rushes where it has built its nest and only secondarily the side facing the water. The territories of birds nesting in the vegetation beside rivers and streams are similar in form. Songbirds nesting in unbroken woods have a roughly circular territory. Several birds of different species can have their nesting territories in a single habitat, since, as emphasized above, competition for space occurs only between birds of the same species. The Blackbird and the Robin can both nest in the territory of the Mistle Thrush, for example, and all three can have their small territories inside the wide domain of a single pair of Sparrowhawks.

The size of nesting territories also shows considerable geographical variability. In Germany, a pair of woodpeckers inhabits an area of approximately 4,000,000 sq m, in Holland 8,500,000 sq m and in Finland 8,000,000 — 10,000,000 sq m. In these cases, the size of the area evidently depends on the quality and character of the forest vegetation and also, to some extent, on the abundance of the species, although it has been found with small birds that greater population density of the species is not accompanied by a decrease in the size of the territory.

Individual couples of the same species do not trespass on their neighbours' territory, chiefly because every male — and sometimes the female as well — actively defends its domain and loudly proclaims its limits. We must not think that the limits of the territory are represented by a clearly marked line. Small infringements are quite common, if only because it is not possible for the rightful inhabitants to be everywhere all the time and to squabble over every minor offence. The vehemence with which a bird defends its territory is further dependent on the strength of the nesting instinct. Vocal proclamation of the limits of the territory usually suffices to inform neighbours that the next-door plot is occupied. If another individual of the same species appears in the vicinity, the singing bird keeps a sharp eye on it and raises its voice. If you can imitate the spring voice of the Nuthatch, you will see how annoyed it becomes if you start to whistle in its nesting area. It immediately flies closer, ruffles its feathers and looks for the bold intruder who has ventured into its territory.

When rivals meet, they usually put on impressive displays, characterized by special poses and movements, by showing off plumage and colour, and by vocalization. This behaviour is innate and is species specific. The rival's specific behaviour is induced either by the whole complex of these factors, or by only some of them, and the moral effect of the display is usually sufficient to drive the intruder away. In extreme cases of maximum excitement, a battle and chase may occur, but these are generally only symbolic in character. Serious fights, in which feathers fly and blood is shed, are comparatively rare. After driving its rival away, the victor often starts to sing again immediately to assert its supremacy. The defending bird always has a greater moral advantage, and thus greater chances of victory.

The concept of the territory is not completely suppressed even in birds which nest closely packed side by side in large colonies. It is limited to the immediate surrounds of the nest, however, and sometimes only to the distance which the sitting bird can reach with its beak. This explains the smallness of the areas given for the King Penguin and the Black-headed Gull in the table.

There is a number of birds with no territorial instinct, however, and in others the situation is somewhat complex. The nesting area may be much smaller than the food area and, in addition, there may be winter areas and mating areas, as in the case of the Black-headed Gull.

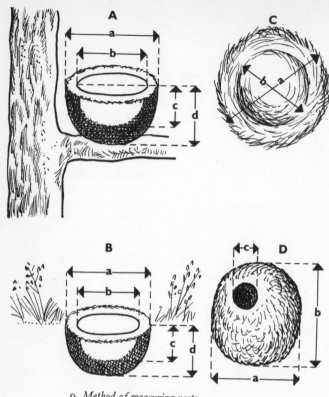

9. *Method of measuring nests*
ABC a — *diameter of nest*, b — *diameter of well*,
c — *depth of well*, d — *height of nest*
D a — *width of nest*, b — *height of nest*, c — *diameter of entrance*

Birds' nests and eggs are interesting and very diverse, but
I should not like this book to rouse the reader's interest in egg-
collecting; it is generally of no real scientific value, and is
harmful to bird preservation. The large show collections of

individual eggs possessed by some amateur ornithologists have no scientific significance; valuable zoological collections always contain whole clutches. This way of collecting eggs would have a very harmful effect on bird populations already decimated in this manner, however. It is therefore not surprising that egg-collecting is now illegal in most civilized countries and is permitted only in exceptional cases where it is justified by scientific needs.

In field ornithological studies, every ornithologist, whether professional or amateur, ought to pay special attention to the nest biology of birds, since during the breeding season their instinctive life develops to an almost incredible extent. This gives us an opportunity not only of studying their psychology, but also of learning more about certain problematical phenomena such as the formation of couples, and of becoming acquainted with their instinctive behaviour during nest-building and with their care of the eggs and young. In the present age, when nature is undergoing radical changes, it is important to notice the way in which birds adapt to altered environmental conditions, as the findings can be of value for nature protection. A detailed study of the literature and comparison of the various data would show that, surprisingly, some data are missing altogether — even in the case of very common and numerous species — or that they require verification. This applies, for example, to the part played by the partners in building the nest and incubating the eggs, and to the incubation time. Thus everybody who is interested in bird life has an opportunity of contributing to knowledge of their biology.

On the following pages the reader will find pictures of the nests and eggs of a number of well-known European birds, together with information on their nest biology and on the diversity of the forms, localization and manner of construction of their nests, and will see a few samples of the wide range of coloration and markings of birds' eggs. Since the shape and localization of the nest and the colouring of the eggs may vary considerably in the same species, the commonest types of nests and eggs are illustrated here. For the eggs, the illustrators made use of the exceptionally large oological collection of the National Museum in Prague. They also referred to the nest collection of this museum when illustrating the nests, although in most cases these were studied in their natural surroundings. In a few cases of species with almost inaccessible nests, they were obliged to use original photographs as their models. Since it was not always possible to show the eggs in their natural size, the actual dimensions are always given in the relevant text.

When identifying eggs, their size — which in every species varies within a given range — has to be taken into account, as well as their colouring and shape. In addition to the mean values, we have therefore also given the maximum and minimum values of both basic dimensions (length and width) of the eggs of the individual species.

The Great Crested Grebe
(Podiceps cristatus)

Dimensions of the eggs
(in millimetres):
Mean   — *55.8 × 36.9*
Maxima — *62.7 × 37.8 and 56.4 × 40.2*
Minima — *46.5 × 39 and 50 × 33.5*

The whole structure of the body and the dense, flat plumage indicate that this bird's element is the water. It is an excellent swimmer and dives in search of food. During the breeding season the Great Crested Grebe is found mainly on stagnant water, lakes and ponds, as long as they are bordered by some kind of reeds and rushes. Sometimes the Great Crested Grebe nests on creeks and river arms; in Eastern Europe it also nests on salt and brackish lakes.

The nest is usually concealed in rushes, reeds and sedge. It consists of an untidy heap of aquatic plants, the greater part of which is submerged, leaving only a relatively low, shallow dish for the eggs above the surface. In shallow water, the nest rests on the bottom, as its total height is usually 45—50 cm. In deep water, however, it floats, so that waves may carry it some distance from the original site. The Great Crested Grebe has also been known to build its nest in the middle of a network of aquatic plants right out on the open water. On other occasions nesting colonies have been found in which the individual nests were only a few yards apart.

When first laid, the four to six eggs are bluish-white with a chalky coat, but during incubation contact with rotting vegetation in the nest gives them a brownish tinge. The incubation period is 20—21 days and both parents take turns to sit on the eggs. Whenever the parents leave the nest, they cover the clutch with nest material, probably to hide the eggs from enemies. Decomposition of the vegetable material raises the temperature in the nest, but this, by itself, does not contribute to the incubation of the eggs.

The Little Grebe, or Dabchick
(Podiceps ruficollis)

Dimensions of the eggs (in mm):
Mean — *38 × 26.2*
Maxima — *43 × 27.4 and 31.2 × 28.3*
Minima — *32.8 × 23.7 and 37 × 24*

Unlike its larger relatives of the genus *Podiceps*, the Little Grebe leads a secretive existence in large stretches of aquatic plants. At nesting time it therefore seeks out thickly overgrown arms of ponds, lakes and rivers. Sometimes quite a small area of water — a pool or a small pond — is sufficient if it can find adequate shelter there. It is seldom seen on running water and large lakes. Even when looking for food it prefers to keep to the edge or within the bounds of the reeds and sedge and rarely ventures out on to the open water. It betrays the position of its nest by its frequent and varied calls.

The nest of the Little Grebe is similar in type to that of other closely related members of the genus. Like the Great Crested Grebe, it makes a nest of different and partly rotting aquatic plants. It uses finer material, however, and in accordance with its size, the nest is relatively small (about the size of a plate). In structure and size, the nest resembles that of the Black-necked Grebe *(Podiceps nigricollis)*. While the latter species sometimes nests in colonies, the Little Grebe always nests individually. According to the depth of the water, the nest either rests on the bottom or floats, held firm to the surrounding aquatic plants by their blades. On leaving the nest, the parents cover the eggs. Incubation of the four to seven eggs, which takes 2 weeks, is started as soon as the first one has been laid, both parents taking turns to sit on the clutch. The eggs are coloured like those of other grebes, but are much smaller.

The Fulmar
(Fulmarus glacialis)

Dimensions of the eggs (in mm):
Mean — *74 × 50.6*
Maxima — *81.5 × 50.5 and 72.7 × 54.1*
Minima — *65.5 × 45.5 and 66.5 × 44.3*

The Fulmar is a true bird of the high seas and spends most of its life over the water. The only exception is at breeding time, when it comes ashore or settles on islands in the sea. Its breeding colonies are usually right beside the sea, so that the rocks on which the birds nest are washed by the waves. In arctic regions, however, Fulmar colonies have been found in mountain valleys several miles from the sea.

Fulmars nesting on the British Isles arrive there in individual couples, already paired, between November and February. Laying starts about half-way through May and the eggs are placed either on projecting or shelving rocks, or on softer ground, in a deep hollow lined with a little grass. In some cases the birds deposit a few stones round the eggs.

The female generally lays only one egg, variably oval in shape, with a dull, dingy white shell sparsely marked with small, reddish-brown spots, which are evidently of secondary origin. The male and the female both incubate the eggs and during this time they both have bald brood spots. The data of different observers on the length of the incubation period vary, although in any case it is remarkably long (42—49 or 56—60 days). The young are covered with thick, whitish-grey down and are fed only about twice a day. The nestling pushes its beak, or even its whole head, into the gullet of the parent bird, which regurgitates partly digested food. Young Fulmars remain in the nest 48—57 days and thus do not make their first expeditions out into the open sea until the middle of August.

The Cormorant
(Phalacrocorax carbo)

Dimensions of the eggs (in mm):
Mean   — 63 × 39.4
Maxima — 74 × 41.7 and 68.5 × 44
Minima — 56 × 38.8 and 56.4 × 35.4

This famous diver and successful hunter not unnaturally always nests near water with an abundant supply of fish, as on the seashore, near large rivers and their estuaries, or close to large lakes. Cormorants are proverbially sociable birds and nest in colonies sometimes comprising thousands of couples. Not infrequently they associate with other colony-nesters such as Herons.

The nest is usually built on steep cliffs overlooking the sea or on tall trees, but may occasionally be placed among rushes. It is not uncommon to find several Cormorant nests in the wide top of a single tree. Thick branches form the foundations of the nest, while the superstructure consists of fine, dry twigs usually intermingled with green sprays. The nest is lined with rush, sedge, blades of grass and leaves. The building material is taken from the environment, so that in colonies nesting by the sea it often includes seaweed. Branches are either broken off from trees in the vicinity or are collected from the water. Cormorants constantly add to the nest throughout the whole of the breeding period, sometimes even after the young have been hatched.

A Cormorant pair does not build a new nest every year. If possible, it uses the foundations of an old nest from the previous year and simply adds to it and improves it. Quite often it builds on the abandoned nests of birds of other species, such as herons, crows or birds of prey. The female lays three to five whitish-blue eggs with a typical chalky coat, so that the basic colour is largely invisible. The eggs are incubated for 23—24 days by both parents. Soon after they are hatched, the young climb about among the branches round the nest. They are fed by the adult birds for 30—56 days.

The Heron
(Ardea cinerea)

Dimensions of the eggs (in mm):
Mean   — 61×43
Maxima — 70.6×43 and 61.5×49.7
Minima — 53.5×43.2 and 62×38.9

Herons are also bound by their food requirements to water.
They nest either in the tree-tops or among reeds, in the middle
of extensive swamps or in low shrubs. Both deciduous trees and
conifers are used as nesting sites. The Heron usually nests in
large colonies, but solitary nests are by no means rare. Herons
hunt their prey in shallow water, where their long legs enable
them to wade in comfort or to stand motionless waiting for prey.

The male chooses the site of the nest and starts to build it.
Soon afterwards, following an interesting nuptial ceremony, it
is joined by a female. As the foundation for the nest, Herons
generally employ the nests of other large birds from the previous
year. They pull the old nests apart and use the material to make
new ones. The massive base of the nest is made of thick branches
and clumps of turf, while the top consists of fine branches and
rushes and is lined with small twigs, rootlets, blades of grass,
hairs and reeds. The size of the nest is very variable, completely
new nests being far smaller than those which have been added
to for several years. Herons add to their nests throughout the
whole of the nesting period, fetching the building material in
their beak.

The clutch consists of four to five bluish-green eggs. Since the
eggs are laid at average intervals of two days and the female
starts to brood as soon as the first one has been laid, the young
are hatched successively and vary considerably in size. These
size differences persist throughout the whole of the rearing
period.

The Mallard
(Anas platyrhynchos)

Dimensions of the eggs (in mm):
Mean   —   *56.8×41.2*
Maxima —   *64.5×42.1 and 62.7×47.6*
Minima —   *50×39 and 58.4×35.6*

The Mallard nests near water where it can find at least a little peace and quiet in the waterside vegetation. Its commonest nesting places are shallow lakes, ponds, pools, old creeks and river arms and swamps. The nest may be placed in thick rushes, islands of reed-grass, tall grass or stinging-nettles, or even in a field, often under a bush or a small tree or beside the trunk of a large tree. In some regions the Mallard regularly nests above the ground, for example in holes and hollows in osier willows.

The nest may be situated several miles from the nearest stretch of water, however. In such cases the female leads the young via brooks, canals and ditches to the nearest suitable water and rears the family there. The male plays no part in the rearing of the young, but merely helps to look for a convenient nesting site.

Nests built on the ground are made of different dry parts of plants and are well shaped inside. The duck collects the building material in the vicinity. It lines the nest while nesting with fine down plucked from its own belly. As down is added, the amount increases until the overflow eventually forms a pretty wreath all round the nest. If the clutch is not complete, the female, on leaving the nest, covers it with nest material. The seven to twelve greenish-grey eggs are incubated for 24—28 days. Soon after the young are hatched the female leads them to the water, where they live in the shelter of the aquatic vegetation.

The Teal
(Anas crecca)

Dimensions of the eggs (in mm):
Mean — *44.8 × 32.9*
Maxima — *51.8 × 33.9 and 47.6 × 35.2*
Minima — *41 × 32.9 and 42 × 30*

Like the Mallard, the Teal frequents different types of stagnant inland water whose vegetation provides it with adequate shelter. It even nests near small forest pools. The nest is usually situated close to the water, or right beside it. It is generally very well concealed in sedge, islands of reed-grass, thick clumps of bulrushes or tall grass and is often placed under bushes for better protection. Small islands are very popular nesting places.

The female builds the nest, which is made of vegetable material found in the immediate vicinity. The bird forms a deep, regular well with its breast and faces it with a layer of fine, dry plants. Like other ducks, it lines the nest with delicate dark grey down, which piles up until the nest is finally surrounded by a light, fluffy wreath.

The eight to ten creamy-yellow eggs are incubated by the female for 21—23 days. The nesting habits of the Teal and the way in which it rears its young are largely similar to those of the Mallard.

The young of the Teal, like those of other ducks, are nidifugous and make for the water, accompanied by the female, soon after they are hatched. The male pays no attention to them whatsoever. The whole family remains in the shelter of the vegetation and can be seen in the open only in the early morning and evening when the young busily catch aquatic insects and other small creatures on the surface of the water.

The Tufted Duck
(Aythya fuligula)

Dimensions of the eggs (in mm):
Mean — *59×41*
Maxima — *66.9×41.1 and 63.9×47.2*
Minima — *53×37.8 and 57.8×37.4*

This little black and white duck, which, as its name implies, has a tuft on the back of its head, can be seen on stagnant and slowly running water or even in sea creeks. Since it catches its food on the bottom, it tends to frequent shallow water with gently sloping sides overgrown with rushes, sedge and reed-grass and provided with shade by trees and shrubs. Like the Mallard, it also lives on small ponds and lakes in the parks of some European towns. It usually nests right at the water's edge. The small nest, which resembles the nests of other ducks in structure, is made of the dry parts of plants near the nest. It is faced inside with fine material and is later lined with dark brown downy feathers with a barely discernible light spot in the centre. The Tufted Duck conceals its nest very thoroughly in a thick tangle of aquatic plants, generally in a large stretch of reed-grass, reeds and other grasses. Very often the site is an island of reed-grass surrounded by water. It is very unusual for the nest to be more than 100 m from the water. Low islands make a particularly satisfactory nesting place and on these we may find several nests close together, thus constituting a rudimentary colony.

If they have an opportunity, Tufted Ducks are very fond of nesting inside, or at the edge of, gull and tern colonies, possibly because they feel safer there, as these birds are very sensitive to the slightest danger. The clutch contains eight to ten, and sometimes twelve, eggs. If there are more than this number in the nest, they come, as a rule, from two or more ducks.

The Mute Swan
(Cygnus olor)

Dimensions of the eggs (in mm):
Mean   —   *112.8×73.5*
Maxima   —   *122×77.1 and 119×80*
Minimum —   *99×68*

The Mute Swan is found in many parts of Europe. These are mostly tame or half-tame, artificially bred birds, however. The original home of wild swans is Northern Europe.

We can distinguish differences in the nesting habits of tame, half-tame and wild swans, as tame birds are often content with a small lake in a park and frequently nest in places which would never be used by the wild variety. Feral or wild swans living under natural conditions nest only by large stretches of water such as lakes, large ponds, wide river arms or deltas with a deep border of vegetation.

The nest is generally well concealed by vegetation and is situated either on the ground, or in shallow water, with the base resting on the bottom. It is a more or less spherical pile of branches, bulrush and reed stems, etc., up to 0.5 m high. The foundations measure 1.5−2 m across and the inside of the nest 40−45 cm. The lining consists of extremely fine dry and wet material, among which we always find isolated, white, downy feathers. The nest is usually not far from open water. The adult birds generally use the same route to get to the water, thus forming a kind of corridor in which the aquatic plants are bent and broken.

The Buzzard
(Buteo buteo)

Dimensions of the eggs (in mm):
Mean   —   *55 × 40*
Maxima -   *62.5 × 47.1 and 59 × 49*
Minima — *49.8 × 40.2 and 51 × 39.1*

The Buzzard is one of the commonest birds of prey and since it is a sworn foe of small rodents, it deserves our full protection. It nests in unbroken coniferous, deciduous and mixed forests at low and high altitudes. In Britain it also nests on rocky coasts. However, it hunts its prey in open country (fields, meadows and pastures). The Buzzard builds its nest in trees, usually beside the trunk, but sometimes on a branch, 10—20 m above the ground. It only nests on rocks and hillsides in unwooded country.

The nest is a huge structure 60—85 cm across, built on a foundation of thick branches. The superstructure is made of thin branches and the shallow basin is lined with grass, leaves, conifer twigs, bark, moss and fur. We can usually find fresh green twigs or conifer sprays on the nest. Buzzards build their own nests. If they use an old one from the previous year, they always add to it, so that a nest which has been employed for several years attains a considerable height. The Buzzard seldom uses an abandoned nest belonging to another species. It is interesting that it is very slow in forming and lining the inside of the nest and does not start to raise the edges until after the young have been hatched.

The female lays two to four dull, white eggs with mauvish-grey and often delicate pink, deep spots, and yellowish-brown, brown or chocolate-brown surface spots. The parent birds both take turns to sit on the eggs, but the female's part in this activity is greater than the male's. The same applies to the feeding of the young, in which the male's role is chiefly to fetch food.

The Sparrowhawk
(Accipiter nisus)

Dimensions of the eggs (in mm):
Mean   —   *40 × 32*
Maxima —   *46.7 × 35 and 45.5 × 36*
Minima —   *34 × 28.3 and 34 × 28.3*

As distinct from the Buzzard, which likes coherent forests, the Sparrowhawk prefers to nest in regions where small woods alternate with open country. Its favourite haunts are coniferous rather than deciduous woods. It likes spruce growths near streams or groups of spruce firs surrounded by deciduous or mixed growths. If better accommodation is lacking, it will also nest in pines, silver firs and deciduous trees.

The nest, which is made of dry branches and is usually built close to the trunk, varies in size according to whether it is new or has already been used several times. A new nest takes about 15 days to build and the work is done by both mates. It is 25—40 cm in diameter and the relatively deep well (5—7 cm), is 15—20 cm across. It is usually situated half-way up the branched part of the tree, 3—8 m above the ground, and is roofed over with green branches. Inside it is lined with small twigs, pieces of bark, needles, moss, hairs and sometimes small feathers. The Sparrowhawk also completes the construction of its nest during nesting. A couple of Sparrowhawks will sometimes use an old crow's, pigeon's or Jay's nest, or even a squirrel's nest, which they adapt by simply adding to it.

The female lays four to six oval, bluish-white eggs with mauvish-grey deep spots and dark brown or chocolate-brown surface spots. They are incubated only by the female, while the male goes hunting and brings food.

The Kestrel
(Falco tinnunculus)

Dimensions of the eggs (in mm):
Mean — 37.8 × 31.1
Maxima — 47.2 × 30.7 and 41.5 × 34.2
Minima — 35.4 × 29.7 and 34 × 27.5

The Kestrel is one of the commonest birds of prey. We can recognize it by its fluttering wings as it hovers, poised in the air, while keeping a look-out for its prey, which consists of small rodents such as voles and mice. It therefore occurs in open country where hunting is easier.

Kestrels have two types of nesting sites — trees or steep rocks and precipices. Like a number of birds which nest on rocks, the Kestrel has also taken to nesting on high towers, in ruins and on tall buildings, often in the centre of large towns. It avoids the depths of large forests and when it nests in trees it chooses a small group of trees standing in a field or on the outskirts of a wood.

The Kestrel does not build its own nest, but uses the abandoned nests of crows, pigeons, Magpies and various birds of prey, so that description of its nest is impossible. It chooses nests as high as possible — usually 12—20 m — above the ground. On rocks, it nests in fissures or holes or on jutting ledges. The female lays five to seven yellowish-white eggs strikingly marked with reddish-brown spots, sometimes so thickly that the basic colour is practically invisible. The way in which the eggs are incubated varies. Sometimes only the female sits on them, sometimes it is relieved from time to time by the male. The task of hunting and fetching food is always the duty of the male, however. The incubation period is 28—31 days.

The Pheasant
(Phasianus colchicus)

Dimensions of the eggs (in mm):
Mean — *45.1 × 35.6*
Maxima — *50 × 35.5 and 48 × 39*
Minima — *39 × 36.5 and 41 × 32.1*

The Pheasant originally came from the area extending from the east of the Black Sea across the whole southern part of palaearctic Asia, where numerous geographical races are to be found. Since the Middle Ages, when it was introduced into a few European countries, it has become thoroughly acclimatized and now forms an integral and familiar part of the European fauna. It inhabits lowlands and hillocks, chiefly in open country where forests alternate with fields and light mixed woods with thickets, copses and riverside woods. It has a special predilection for water thickly surrounded by shrubs and rushes.

Pheasants are polygamous and each male has several females. Consequently, the care of the eggs and young is entirely the concern of the female. The nest is a shallow hollow in the ground, sometimes concealed by the branches of shrubs or the higher leaves and blades of grass, stinging nettles and other plants. It is very rare to find the Pheasant nesting in the middle of a cultivated field. The nest is always situated so that the female has a free way of escape in case of danger. It is only sparsely lined with dry blades of grass and leaves.

The single-coloured eggs are olive-brown, greyish-green or greyish-blue. They are relatively glossy and are only roughly oval. The clutch contains eight to fifteen eggs, the rule being for young females to lay fewer eggs than older birds. The female usually does not start to brood until the last egg has been laid and incubates them for 24—25 days. The young are nidifugous and soon after being hatched they start to look for their own food, guided by the female.

The Moorhen
(*Gallinula chloropus*)

Dimensions of the eggs (in mm):
Mean — 43.8 × 30.6
Maxima — 54 × 31.5 and 46 × 34.2
Minima — 35.3 × 29.8 and 36.2 × 26

There is surely hardly a stretch of water bordered by rushes, sedge, reed-grass and other aquatic plants which does not harbour this interesting bird of the rail family (Rallidae). It nests beside offshoots of large ponds and even by tiny ponds and pools, overgrown canals and flooded pit shafts and is likewise found in river creeks. It has also been reported to nest near brackish water. Moorhens do not venture out on to open water, but remain either in the vegetation or at its periphery, from where their sonorous calls can often be heard.

A pair of Moorhens usually builds several nests, but employs only one of them for rearing the young. The nest is generally situated above or near the water and is concealed by the water-side vegetation, which also constitutes the building material. In isolated cases the nests of other aquatic birds are used as a foundation. It is quite common to find a Moorhen's nest on dry ground among osiers.

The foundations of the nest consist of twigs and dry blades and leaves of rushes and other plants, while the superstructure is made of the finer parts of plant leaves, small roots and blades of grass. The well is 15—25 cm across and 10—15 cm deep and quite often contains an admixture of the green parts of plants. Both the parent birds continue to improve the nest while brooding. The seven to ten eggs are yellow, with blackish-brown and black spots, and both parents participate in their incubation, which takes 19—22 days.

The Coot
(Fulica atra)

Dimensions of the eggs (in mm):
Mean   — 52.5 × 35.8
Maxima — 59.7 × 38 and 59.6 × 40
Minima — 44.2 × 33.1 and 44.2 × 33.1

Like the Moorhen, the Coot generally inhabits overgrown lakes, ponds, pools and quiet creeks. Its nest is to be found mainly in the middle of rushes, sedge and other aquatic plants, although it does not require such thick growths as the Moorhen. The bird always leaves itself free access from the nest to the water and seldom builds on dry ground. There are exceptions, however, and ornithological literature contains descriptions of nests situated in meadows or fields several metres away from the water. Near the main nest the Coot sometimes builds a number of small ones, which are used by the young as sleeping nests.

The true nest is 15—20 cm high and is made of the dry stems and leaves of rushes, reeds and other aquatic plants. It either floats on the water, anchored to the surrounding plants, or rests on the bottom. The Coot often makes a kind of arch of leaves and blades, broken off from rushes growing in the vicinity, over the nest, to hide it from the eyes of foes. The shallow well is only occasionally lined with finer material. Access to the water is facilitated by a sort of low bridge built by the bird from the same material as the nest. Both the mates participate in the building of the nest.

The seven to ten eggs are dull and are marked with small purple spots on a yellowish-grey ground. The adult birds take turns to sit on the eggs which are incubated for 21—24 days. The nidifugous young leave the nest successively as soon as their feathers are dry and are led by the male until they are joined by the last one. After that, both the parent birds look after them.

The Lapwing
(*Vanellus vanellus*)

Dimensions of the eggs (in mm):
Mean — *46.5 × 33.4*
Maxima — *58 × 32.5 and 47.4 × 37.2*
Minima — *41 × 30.4 and 46.8 × 30*

The Lapwing is a familiar inhabitant of wet meadows and water-logged fields near water. Since swampy meadows are drained and cultivated, the Lapwing has had to learn to adapt itself to relatively dry terrains and sometimes nests directly in fields. We can often find its nests on wet or dry mud at the side of ponds, lakes or flat river deltas.

The male Lapwing chooses the site for the nest and performs its striking nuptial flights above it, to the accompaniment of plaintive calls. Making shallow hollows with its breast is part of its courting technique. The female selects one of these hollows and lines it meagrely with stems, blades of grass, leaves and pieces of wood found in the immediate neighbourhood, to form a nest. Nests on waterlogged ground are generally higher and better lined than nests built on dry ground.

The Lapwing starts to nest very early in the spring, when the vegetation is usually still undeveloped, so that the sitting bird can be seen from a considerable distance. As soon as it catches sight of a potential enemy, it runs a little way away from the nest, keeping close to the ground, and only then raises itself erect. The nest and eggs are hard to find, as they blend perfectly with their surroundings. The eggs have good protective colouring, being olive-grey thickly speckled with brownish-black spots, particularly at the blunt end. As with all waders, there are usually four in a clutch and they lie in the nest with the pointed end facing inwards Lapwings' eggs were once collected as a great delicacy. The adult birds both participate in the incubation of the eggs, but the part played by the male is much smaller. The incubation period is about 24 days.

The Snipe
(Gallinago gallinago)

Dimensions of the eggs (in mm):
Mean   — 39.6 × 28.5
Maxima — 42.9 × 29 and 39.6 × 31
Minima — 35 × 28.4 and 36.8 × 26.7

The Snipe inhabits reed-grass swamps, waterlogged meadows, the wet, overgrown sides of lakes and ponds, river deltas and upland peat-bogs. It would not be correct to say that the presence of open water is absolutely essential to it during the nesting period, but it is not so adaptable as the Lapwing, however. If the swamps or wet meadows are drained, the Snipe disappears. It looks for food by prodding the ground with its long beak, and for this the ground needs to be soft and boggy.

The nest is generally situated close to the place over which the male performs its typical nuptial flights. During flight the bird suddenly plunges headlong, to the accompaniment of a bleating sound produced by the vibrations of its spread outer tail feathers. The nest is usually very well concealed in a clump of grass or an island of reed-grass. It consists of a simple hollow very sparsely lined with different dry parts of plants. Although the Snipe adds to it during nesting, it is seldom more than 3 cm thick.

Only the female is responsible for incubating the four eggs. They resemble the eggs of other waders in shape, are sharply pointed and always lie in the nest with the pointed end facing inwards. Their ground colour is olive-green or olive-yellow and they are marked with dull grey, deep spots and dark brown surface spots. The female, which sits on the eggs for 19—21 days, leaves the nest only in the presence of immediate danger.

The Curlew
(Numenius arquata)

Dimensions of the egg₀ (in mm):
Mean — *67.8×47.5*
Maxima — *82.6×52.7 and 78.6×55.1*
Minima — *56×43 and 56.6×41.7*

The Curlew is another wader. It nests in wide, flat terrains, such as waterlogged meadows, swamps, peat-bogs and moors, but is also to be found in comparatively dry places, as long as there is water close by. It has even been known to nest on sandy sites with low vegetation near the sea. During the breeding season the males perform beautiful nuptial flights and utter curious melodious calls.

Like other waders, the Curlew nests in a simple hollow in the ground, generally in places with a good view. The courting couple usually form several such hollows with their bodies, but use only one of them. The nest is about 20 cm across and is meagrely lined with blades of grass and stems.

As a rule, the female lays four eggs, at intervals of 1—3 days. The eggs are olive-green or olive-brown and are sprinkled with grey deep spots and dark greenish-brown surface spots. The spots are thicker at the blunt end of the egg. The parents share in the incubation of the eggs, which takes 26—28 days. Soon after they are hatched, the young leave the nest to explore their surroundings and are very skilled at hiding in the tangled vegetation, especially if in danger. In such cases the worried adult birds circle round the intruder and by their constant calls try to draw attention to themselves.

The Redshank
(Tringa totanus)

Dimensions of the eggs (in mm):
Mean — *44.8 × 31.2*
Maxima — *48.5 × 31.1 and 44.7 × 33.4*
Minimum — *40.8 × 28.5*

The melodious call of the Redshank can be heard during the nesting season in wet places inland and also near the coast. It nests in open country, in meadows beside lakes, ponds and running water, in river deltas and by the sea. It does not like meadows with tall vegetation, however. Sometimes it is content with a peat-bog and sometimes with a grassy spot near a small pool or overgrown water, or with a small patch of waterlogged, grassy ground. The male has a melodious call of several syllables, but in the spring it also utters clear trills during its nuptial flight, in which the bird flies high above its nesting site, with only the tips of its wings quivering. Long before the female starts to lay the eggs, the male chooses a damp spot well hidden by grass and reeds, where it forms a relatively deep hollow, which the female lines with dry grass blades and leaves. It often camouflages the nest by covering it with a kind of roof made of grass and reed blades. In April or May, and occasionally in June (a substitute clutch), the female lays four small, glossy, grey or greyish-yellow eggs marked with separate, ash-grey, deep spots and dark brown surface spots of varying sizes, which often merge with each other. Both parents participate in the incubation of the eggs (22—25 days) and the rearing of the young.

The Common Sandpiper
(Tringa hypoleucos)

Dimensions of the eggs (in mm):
Mean — *36.1 × 25.8*
Maxima — *40.2 × 26.6 and 39 × 27.9*
Minima — *32.8 × 25.3 and 36.9 × 24.8*

During the breeding season this little wader is found mainly near streams and rivers, with low muddy or gravelly banks bordered with shrubs and trees. Sometimes it nests beside river creeks, lakes and dams. It chiefly frequents hilly and mountainous regions and is often encountered in water in the middle of forests. The couples build solitary nests, at some distance from one another, and betray their nesting site by their nuptial flights, which are performed close to the surface of the water and are accompanied by clear, resonant calls.

The nest is a relatively deep hollow in mud or sand, lined with dry leaves or blades of grass. It is usually well concealed under the wide leaves of waterside plants or below the branches of shrubs, either near to or at some distance from the open water. Sometimes it· is completely surrounded by water. As a rule, round the occupied nest we can find other nest hollows formed during the nuptials.

Like other waders, the Common Sandpiper generally lays four eggs. These are glossy and are sometimes a dull, bluish-grey colour, but are most often yellowish-red, and are covered with bluish-grey deep spots and small, reddish-brown surface spots and dots. They are laid at intervals of 1—2 days. Both the parent birds share in their incubation (21—22 days) and in the rearing of the young, but the female plays the greater part in the care of the young. If the clutch is destroyed by high water, a substitute clutch is laid. The nesting period is from May to June.

The Great Black-backed Gull
(Larus marinus)

Dimensions of the eggs (in mm):
Mean   — 76.6 × 53.8
Maxima   — 82.1 × 53.3 and 77 × 57
Minimum — 69.4 × 49

This is the largest member of the gull family and, as implied by its Latin name, it is a marine bird. It likes to nest on cliffs, on gravelly sites or on low islands overgrown with grass or shrubs, not too far from the shore. Sometimes, however, especially in Northern Europe, it nests beside freshwater lakes and large rivers or brackish water within easy reach of the sea. At other times of the year, however, it ranges far from its nesting places.

Like most sea birds it forms large nesting colonies, either alone or together with other sea birds, such as the Herring Gull. Nevertheless, solitary nesting is by no means rare. In May the couples start to build a new nest or to repair an old one. The nest is a relatively large structure made of different parts of plants and wood. It is usually lined with feathers and is sometimes surrounded by stones or fragments of branches. The outer diameter of the nest is 60—70 cm, the height 15—20 cm and the inner diameter 20—25 cm.

In May or June, over a period of 3—4 days, the female usually lays three, but sometimes two or four, eggs of variable colour. The commonest coloration is brown or olive-brown, with grey and yellowish-brown spots. The eggs are incubated for 26—28 days by both parents. Brooding starts with the laying of the first egg, so that the young are hatched successively and vary somewhat in size. They are fed by both parents and are not fledged until they are 45 days old.

The Herring Gull
(Larus argentatus)

Dimensions of the eggs (in mm):
Mean   — *70.5 × 49.1*
Maxima   — *82.7 × 53.7 and 78 × 54.8*
Minimum — *58.5 × 44.1*

The Herring Gull is a coastal bird and forms large nesting colonies anywhere on steep and rocky, but also flat and sandy shores, with or without vegetation. During the nesting season it is not completely bound to the sea — in Asia, for example, it also nests beside lakes and at the mouths of large rivers. The colonies sometimes comprise several hundred pairs, although solitary nesting is not exceptional. Nest-building is preceded by interesting nuptial rites which continue while the eggs are being incubated.

The nest is built by both partners and is made of dry grass. It may be completely new or may be a last year's nest refurbished. The work takes about 3 days and the material is obtained from the immediate vicinity. The finished structure is 50—70 cm across and up to 27 cm high and the feather-lined well is 25 cm across. The nest is either placed in the open, or is protected by clumps of grass and shrubs.

Between the end of March and the beginning of June the female lays usually three, but occasionally two or four, eggs of somewhat variable colouring. Most frequently they are olive or yellowish-brown and are speckled with dark grey deep spots and blackish-brown surface spots, streaks and dots. The average time of incubation (in which both parents take turns to sit on the eggs) is 26 days and the young are hatched at intervals of 1—2 days. After a day or two the young leave the nest and seek shelter against the hot sun and inclement weather among the vegetation. At feeding time the parents summon them with a special call. They are fledged at 6 weeks.

The Common Gull
(*Larus canus*)

Dimensions of the eggs (in mm):
Mean   — 56.2×40.8
Maxima — 64.8×41.3 and 64.4×45
Minima — 53.3×41 and 56.4×36

The Common Gull is not an exclusively marine bird, as it nests beside both salt and fresh water. It nests on hillocks and mounds and prefers either rocky or grassy sites on the seashore or beside lakes and rivers. It is less gregarious than other gulls, its colonies are smaller and solitary nesting is commoner. The nest, which is built in 2—3 days by both partners, is made of dry twigs, blades of grass and leaves, aquatic plants, moss, lichen, etc. The outer diameter of the nest is usually 20—30 cm and the height 3—7 cm, but its form is rather variable, according to where it is situated. For instance, in damp places the foundations of the nest are higher.

Like the other species of gulls, the Common Gull nests only once a year, between April and June. The clutch usually contains three eggs, but often two and occasionaly four or five. The eggs are laid at intervals of 1½—5 days. As with most species of gulls, their colour is very variable. They may be grey, olive-grey or brown, or even greenish or light blue, with dark brown spots and streaks. They are incubated 26—28 days and the parent birds relieve each other every 2—3 hours. As a rule, brooding does not start until the clutch is complete. At the age of 3—5 days the young leave the nest, but do not wander very far away. Their development takes 57—60 days to complete. Losses among the eggs and young are comparatively high, mainly owing to plundering by large species of gulls.

The Black-headed Gull
(*Larus ridibundus*)

Dimensions of the eggs (in mm):
Mean   — 52.6 × 37
Maxima — 60 × 41.3 and 58.5 × 42.1
Minima — 46 × 38.6 and 49 × 31.2

Although the Black-headed Gull occasionally nests on the coast, it must nevertheless be regarded as an inland bird, as it nests mainly beside stagnant water or slow-flowing fresh water bordered by a thick belt of rushes and reed-grass. Its colonies, which vary in size from a few to several thousand couples, are to be found beside quiet offshoots of lakes, near ponds, in river creeks or on small, low islands. Beside the sea, it nests in similar spots, or on sandy or rocky eminences.

The nest may be placed on firm ground, or among aquatic plants, so that it is surrounded by water. It is built by both birds and is made of the blades and leaves of rushes, reed-grass, etc. Nests built in water are large structures, the foundations of which rest on the bottom, while nests which lie on firm ground sometimes consist of nothing more than a few reed blades carelessly thrown together.

The complete clutch generally comprises three eggs. If there are more than four eggs in the nest, they belong to two females. The basic colour is usually rusty-green and the markings consist of grey deep spots and dark brown surface spots. Eggs are also found with pale blue or red as the ground colour. The adult birds take turns to incubate the eggs and do not start to brood until the last one has been laid. The young are hatched in 22—24 days. They remain a few days in the nest, covered by the parent bird's body, and then leave it to hide in the vegetation round the nest. They are capable of independent flight at about 6 days. They are fed by both the parent birds.

The Kittiwake
(Rissa tridactyla)

Dimensions of the
eggs (in mm):
Mean   — *56.6 × 41.2*
Maximum — *60.8 × 43.2*
Minimum — *47.1 × 35.3*

While nesting, and for a large part of the rest of the year, the Kittiwake is bound to the sea and it is one of the few regular inhabitants of the famous bird islands. Its breeding colonies often comprise several thousand couples. It seldom forms small groups and very rarely nests inland.

The Kittiwake builds its nests on inaccessible jutting rocks and ledges. It is constructed by both the male and the female from moss and seaweed or other aquatic plants. It is very strong, as the birds reinforce the edges with excreta or mud. In narrow rock fissures it can be as much as 100 cm high. The outer diameter is 25—30 cm and the inner diameter 15—20 cm. The Kittiwake also uses old nests, which it simply refurbishes and enlarges. Kittiwakes return to the same colony every year and one couple probably uses the same nest several times. Old, frequently used nests can weigh as much as 10 kg.

The female lays two, or occasionally three, eggs, usually at the end of May or the beginning of June. Substitute clutches often contain only one egg. The eggs are dull and of a coarse texture. They are marked, on a greyish-yellow, red-tinged or brownish ground, with ash-grey and mauvish-grey deep spots and yellowish- to blackish-brown surface spots, not very thickly distributed. The eggs are incubated for 21—24 days by both the parent birds. The young are not fully fledged until they are 4—5 weeks old and for the whole of this time they are fed by the parents. Even afterwards the adult birds still look after them for a short period.

The Common Tern
(Sterna hirundo)

Dimensions of the eggs (in mm):
Mean — 41.6 × 30.1
Maxima — 45.9 × 29.1 and 42.2 × 32.5
Minima — 35.7 × 28.3 and 41.6 × 25

The Common Tern frequents the banks of flowing and stagnant inland waters. As a rule, it approaches the sea only as far as the mouths of rivers or lagoons. It usually founds its colonies on arms of mud or sand, close to the water level. If the water rises, the whole colony may be destroyed. Small islands with sparse, low vegetation are another frequent site for tern colonies. Terns return from their summer quarters in South Africa at the end of April and the beginning of May and quickly occupy their old colonies. This is accompanied by interesting nuptial rites between the individual couples, which take place on the ground and in the air. Terns nest either in separate colonies, or together with kindred species and with gulls, although separate groups are more common.

During the nuptials, the male forms a number of nest hollows, one of which is chosen by the female for the eggs. The nest is very modestly lined with dry blades of grass and leaves, or with small twigs. On wet ground it may be as much as 20 cm high. Between the second half of May and the beginning of June, the female lays about three eggs (occasionally two to five). The eggs are brownish- or greyish-green and are covered with large, grey deep spots and smaller, dark brown surface spots.

Most of the brooding is done by the female. The young are hatched in 20—23 days and a few hours later they already leave the nest and hide in its vicinity. During the first days they still return to the nest and at 30 days they are capable of flight. This is not the end of the parents' responsibility, however, as right up to the time of migration (the end of August and the beginning of September), they still go on feeding the young.

The Arctic Tern
(Sterna paradisea)

Dimensions of the eggs (in mm):
Mean — *40.2×29.3*
Maxima — *47×24 and 45.8×33.6*
Minima — *35.5×28 and 36.6×27.4*

The Arctic Tern returns to its regular breeding places at the end of April. It is one of the greatest travellers among the birds. Recovery of ringed birds has shown that they migrate from their Arctic nesting sites, following the sea-board, as far as the Antarctic. When they return, they are already paired off. The nuptial rites then commence and two or three weeks later they start to nest. Occasionally they nest inland, beside lakes and rivers, while in Arctic regions they regularly nest in the tundra.

Most of the nesting colonies of the Arctic Tern are found by the sea. The site is usually a flat arm of mud or sand, or a patch of gravel right beside the sea, preferably with low grass or some other vegetation. In colonies, in which the Arctic Tern often nests together with other terns, its nests are further apart than those of the Common Tern, for example. The nest hollow, which measures 10 cm across, is sometimes so shallow that it can hardly be distinguished from the rest of the ground. Arctic Terns usually lay their eggs on the bare ground, but sometimes they give it a modest lining of blades of grass and seaweed, or even of tiny shells or stones. When nesting on a rocky base, the bird lines the nest with moss, sometimes brought from a considerable distance.

The Arctic Tern nests in May and June. The clutch generally consists of two eggs very similar in coloration to those of the Common Tern. The main colour is grey, olive or brown and the markings are blackish-brown spots, which often run into each other. During the incubation period (21—22 days), both parents sit on the eggs, but the female spends longer on them than the male. Like other terns, the Arctic Tern nests only once a year.

The Little Tern
(Sterna albifrons)

Dimensions of the eggs (in mm):
Mean — *32.3 × 23.8*
Maxima — *36.4 × 23.5 and 31.7 × 25.3*
Minima — *29.1 × 22 and 30.6 × 22*

This small tern is to be found during the breeding season beside the sea and near inland waters. As a rule, it does not join the large colonies of other terns, but founds its own small colonies in quiet, remote spots, on arms of sand and mud in rivers and lakes, near the mouths of rivers and streams flowing into the sea and on flat islands. It generally chooses stony or sandy spots without any vegetation. The nest is a simple hollow formed by the female. Sometimes it is unlined and sometimes it is lined with dry grass or fragments of conch shells. If the nest is flooded, the birds nest again. The eggs are laid at the end of May and the beginning of June. There are usually two (seldom three or four) and the parents take turns to sit on them during the incubation period, which lasts 20—22 days. The male sits on them less than the female, but brings the female food. The eggs are sandy-yellow or yellowish-brown and are covered with mauvish-grey deep spots and relatively small, blackish-brown surface spots. Their colouring is very variable, like that of the eggs of other terns, so that there are bluish, single-coloured eggs or unwontedly dark ones. After the young are hatched, the parents remove the shells from the nest. The young leave the nest only a few hours after hatching and never return. For a few more days the adult birds protect the young with their body and sometimes try to tempt them into newly formed nests. The young develop very quickly and are able to fly unaided at the age of 15—17 days.

The Razorbill
(*Alca torda*)

Dimensions of the eggs (in mm):
Mean   — *74.9 × 47.3*
Maxima — *82.4 × 44.1 and 75.9 × 52.4*
Minima — *63.5 × 44.7 and 68.1 × 44*

The Razorbill inhabits some of the coasts round the North Atlantic. It is a typical marine bird and spends most of its life on the surface of the sea. At breeding time, however, it always returns to its nesting place in one of the famous colonies where thousands of nesting birds are packed close together, side by side. As a rule, it chooses steep cliffs or rocky islands, where it often consorts with Guillemots or some species of gulls. It usually forms small communities at the periphery of other bird colonies, but sometimes builds solitary nests 50—100 m apart.

Razorbills return to their nesting places early in the spring, as soon as the weather permits. They nest once a year, the female laying a single pear-shaped egg in May or June. The egg is laid on bare ground or rock, usually at the edge of a fissure or cavity. Sometimes the adult birds place a few loose blades of grass or stones round it.

The egg is dull, has a relatively rough shell and its colouring is unusually variable. It can be whitish, brown or greenish. The deep spots are dull grey and the surface spots chocolate-brown or blackish-brown. The egg is incubated by both the parent birds for 26—35 days. The young bird takes 2—3 days to emerge from the egg. At the age of about 19—20 days, although not fully fledged and with undeveloped primaries ('hand' feathers), it glides or falls into the sea. The parents still guide it, but no longer feed it. Young Razorbills are able to dive well and look for their food themselves.

The Guillemot
(Uria aalge)

Dimensions of the eggs (in mm):
Mean   — 80.7 × 49.4
Maxima — 89.5 × 52.9 and 80 × 53
Minima   — 73.8 × 46.4 and 84.1 × 43.8

The Guillemot is a typical inhabitant of sea bird colonies on steep cliffs and islands in the Atlantic and Pacific oceans. It is usually the most numerous species in such colonies. Its neighbours are auks, Razorbills, Kittiwakes, petrels and shearwaters. When not nesting, part of the colony remains on the sea over a wide radius round the nest, while other members fly southwards, as far as the Canary Islands and the Mediterranean. Guillemots arrive in their nesting places at the end of April or the beginning of May and the choice of a nesting site generally involves squabbles.

Like the Razorbill, the Guillemot does not build a nest. The single egg is laid at the end of May or the beginning of June on bare rock or a thin layer of soil on a rocky promontory or ledge, or in a fissure. At the beginning of the nesting period, many eggs fall and are lost during fights or when the birds leave their ledges, which are sometimes only 20 cm wide. They do not fall so easily as other birds' eggs, however, as they are pear-shaped and the shell is thicker at the pointed end. If the egg is lost, the birds will nest a second or third time, but otherwise Guillemots nest only once a year.

Guillemots' eggs have very variable colouring. They are always dull and the main colour can vary from dark green or bluish-green to light brown or white. The markings — blackish-brown or russet spots and scrolls — are often thicker at the blunt end. The adult birds incubate the egg for 28—36 days, relieving each other at regular intervals. The young bird leaves the nest at the age of 3—4 weeks, before it is fully fledged, by jumping into the water or on to the beach.

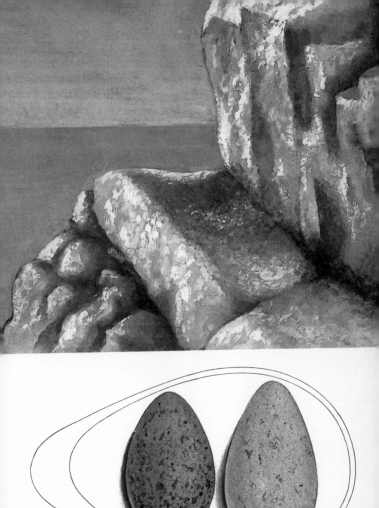

The Stock Dove
(Columba oenas)

Dimensions of the eggs (in mm):
Mean — *37 × 27.7*
Maxima — *43 × 30.3 and 36 × 31*
Minimum — *33.5 × 26.5*

The Stock Dove is the only European member of the pigeon family to nest in tree-hollows. It inhabits coherent deciduous, mixed and coniferous woods in which it can find old, hollow trees. It is commonest at moderate altitudes, but is also encountered in deciduous forests in the lowlands and half-way up mountain sides. In Western Europe it has started to grow accustomed to the presence of man and will nest in old gardens, groups of trees and avenues on the outskirts of built-up areas.

For its nesting site it chooses natural holes formed in rotting trunks or by the breaking off of a thick branch, and also old woodpecker holes. It will sometimes settle in the old nests of birds of prey or crows, in artificial nesting boxes and even in rabbit burrows. In the Balkans it nests in holes in the walls of sand- and clay-pits. The lining of the nest is determined by its size. In the relatively narrow space of woodpecker holes it is sparse, while in roomy artificial nesting boxes it forms a thick layer. Blades of grass, twigs, leaves, small roots, moss and lichen are used.

As a rule, the Stock Dove nests twice a year, though occasionally three or even four times, from the end of March to the beginning of August. Each time it uses a new hole. The eggs (usually only two) take 2—3 days to lay and are incubated in turn by the parent birds for 16—17 days. They are white, glossy and regularly elliptical. Up to the eighth or tenth day the young are blind and are fed on a special secretion from the adult birds' crop known as 'pigeon's milk'. After that they are given vegetable food. They remain in the nest 20—30 days.

The Wood Pigeon
(Columba palumbus)

Dimensions of the eggs
(in mm):
Mean   — 40.1 × 28.7
Maximum — 47.8 × 33
Minimum — 45.6 × 32.2

The Wood Pigeon lives in lowland and mountain forests. It is not fussy in its choice and will nest in any type of wood. It is found more frequently on the outskirts than in the depths of dense forests, however. During the past hundred years or so, in Western Europe it has shown an increasing tendency to nest in town parks and in some places it is now a familiar sight there. The nest is a plain, untidy structure made of various types of twigs. It is so simple that we can often see into it from below. Occasionally the Wood Pigeon nests in the abandoned nests of crows, birds of prey or squirrels.

In deciduous trees the nest is generally placed on a lateral branch, while in conifers it is usually situated beside the trunk, 5—20 m above the ground. It is 30—40 cm across and 7—14 cm high and the well is 3—5 cm deep. There is no special lining. The Wood Pigeon nests twice a year (in rare cases three times). The breeding period lasts from May to July, but may occasionally be extended to August. The female lays two white, glossy, oval eggs.

Both the parent birds participate in the incubation of the eggs, the male usually relieving the female during the middle of the day. The young are hatched in 16—18 days. For about 10 days they are blind and the parents keep them covered up until the fourteenth day. Being typical nidicolous birds, the young remain in the nest and are fed by the parents for 3—4 weeks. After 35 days they are able to fly, but even then they are still fed a little longer by the parents.

The Turtle Dove
(Streptopelia turtur)

Dimensions of the eggs (in mm):
Mean   — 29.9 × 22.8
Maxima — 33.9 × 23.2 and 31.5 × 24.9
Minima — 27 × 21 and 28.6 × 20

The Turtle Dove is found practically everywhere where there are light woods with undergrowth, but it prefers small mixed and deciduous woods to coniferous forests. It will nest in hedges and beside water and marshes if there are shrubs and trees there, and also in small game preserves and old gardens. In Europe it is found at altitudes of up to about 1,000 metres. The nest is placed on horizontal branches in shrubs and trees, 2—6 m above the ground. Like that of the Wood Pigeon, it is a primitive structure consisting of a thin layer of dry twigs, small roots or coarse blades of grass, with spaces in the floor. It measures 20—25 cm across, is 4—5 cm high and has a shallow well.

The work of building the nest is shared by both partners. Old nests of other birds, such as shrikes, thrushes, etc., may be used as the foundation. The first clutch is laid about half-way through May and the nesting period lasts until July. The Turtle Dove nests twice a year. As a rule, the clutch contains two white, glossy, oval eggs.

The adult birds both participate in the incubation of the eggs. The young are hatched in 14—16 days and, like those of other pigeons and doves, are fed on 'milk' secreted in the parents' crop. After about 10 days they are gradually put on to a vegetable diet. They remain in the nest for 18—23 days, but in the event of danger they crawl out on to the surrounding branches much sooner. They are not able to fly until 2—3 days after they have left the nest.

The Barn Owl
(Tyto alba)

Dimensions of the eggs (in mm):
Mean   — *39.8 × 30.6*
Maxima — *45 × 33.4 and 39 × 33.5*
Minima — *36.2 × 31.2 and 37.5 × 28.1*

The Barn Owl inhabits lowlands and small hills and in Europe it is seldom found at altitudes of over 700 m. It nests chiefly in small villages and towns, in ruins, castles, steeples, lofts, etc., and is found in large towns only where it does not have far to go in search of prey. Originally it nested in rocks and is still to be found there in some regions.

The Barn Owl is one of the few birds whose eggs can be found the whole year round. As a rule, the eggs are laid in April or May, but if conditions are favourable, i.e. if there is an abundant food supply, the breeding period may extend from February to November, with the result that we can also find young during the winter. There is usually only one clutch a year, but under favourable conditions there may be two. Conversely, if the supply of small rodents is inadequate, the Barn Owl may not breed at all. It does not make a nest, but lays the eggs on the bare ground. During incubation, a shallow hollow may be formed in the soft earth, or refuse may be piled up to make a rudimentary nest.

The clutch usually contains four to six eggs, although on rare occasions as many as thirteen have been found. Like those of other owls, they are elliptical and are chalky white, finely granular and dull. They are incubated by the female, while the male fetches food. The incubation period is 30—40 days. Since the female lays the eggs at intervals of 1—2 days, the young vary considerably in size. For the first 10—11 days their eyelids are closed and they cannot see. They are fed by both the parents, remain in the nest for 7—9 weeks and are not able to fly until they are about 86 days old.

The Little Owl
(Athene noctua)

Dimensions of the eggs (in mm):
Mean   — *35.6 × 29.5*
Maxima — *39.4 × 28.3 and 37.5 × 31*
Minima — *31 × 28 and 33.5 × 25.7*

This bird occurs in open country at low and moderate altitudes wherever it can find sufficient holes and convenient nesting sites. It avoids large and extensive forests. Its favourite nesting sites are old avenues, parks and gardens, steep rocks and the walls of sand- or clay-pits containing holes and fissures. It is often found in the vicinity of human habitations, where it will nest in remote outbuildings, brickyards, old factories, towers, steeples and ruins.

The Little Owl does not build a nest. Between the beginning of April and the end of May the female lays four or five (occasionally up to eight) eggs on an unpadded base in a hollow tree 3—4 m above the ground, behind a beam in an empty building, in a hole in the wall of a sand- or clay-pit or, in exceptional cases, in the burrow of a rabbit or some other animal, if nothing better is available.

It is rare for the Little Owl to breed more than once a year. The chalky-white eggs are dull, finely grained and widely elliptical or rounded. The female incubates the eggs and evidently does not start to brood until the last one has been laid. The incubation period is 28—29 days. The young are fed by both the parent birds, which also fetch food during the daytime. They remain in the nest for 4—5 weeks and are not able to fly until they are 5 weeks old.

The Tawny Owl
(Strix aluco)

Dimensions of the eggs (in mm):
Mean   — *48.2 × 38.7*
Maxima — *51.7 × 39 and 47 × 40.8*
Minima — *42.3 × 36 and 46.5 × 34.4*

The Tawny Owl is primarily a forest-dweller, but also lives in old avenues, parks and gardens. It prefers deciduous and mixed growths containing old hollow trees or trees with a cavity left by a large decayed or broken branch. If unable to find such accommodation, it will settle in forest hay-lofts, on the floor of hunters' look-out posts, in holes in rocks, in old nests of other birds and even on the ground, beside the trunk of a tree or between the roots. It is very skilled at leaving and entering deep holes in rotting trees and stumps. The Tawny Owl never makes its own nest and lacks the instinct for fetching material and building. As early as December and January we can already hear its hooting calls, which form part of its courting rites, round its nesting sites. As a rule, however, nesting does not actually take place until the middle of March, although it is possible for eggs to be laid in February.

The Tawny Owl normally nests only once a year and lays two to four (on rare occasions up to seven) eggs. The eggs are so roughly elliptical as to be almost spherical; they are white and smooth, with only a faint gloss, and here and there they have small lumps of a chalky substance on the surface. The female lays them at intervals of 2—3 days and starts to incubate them as soon as the first one has been laid. The young are hatched in 28—29 days, at approximately the same intervals as the egg-laying. The male does not take part in incubation, but brings the female food and continues to do so for up to about 10 days after the young are hatched, i.e. for as long as it sits on them. The parents care for the young in the nest for 4—5 weeks, according to the weather and hunting facilities. When the young are able to leave the nest, the parents still look after them for several weeks, until the family finally breaks up.

The Nightjar
(Caprimulgus europaeus)

Dimensions of the eggs (in mm):
Mean   — 31.9 × 22.5
Maxima — 36.5 × 21 and 31.6 × 24.5
Minima — 28.5 × 21.6 and 28.6 × 20

We can see Nightjars hunting and hear their monotonous, growling voice at twilight in warm (usually coniferous) woods at low and moderately high altitudes. Their preserves are usually open spaces, such as clearings, glades, hillocks, moors or sandy areas with little vegetation. They return from their winter quarters in South and East Africa at the end of April or the beginning of May and half-way through May we can already find their eggs.

The Nightjar does not make a nest: the female lays the two eggs on the bare ground. It chooses the most diverse bases for the eggs — stony or sandy soil, fragments of bark, conifer needles or dry leaves. As the bird sits on the eggs, a small hollow is generally formed below them. The 'nest' may be right in the open, or may lie in the shade of a small tree or a bush.

The main colour of the eggs is milky-white or greyish-white and they are covered with two types of spots. The deep spots are light grey, with indistinct edges, and the surface spots are brownish-grey or dark brown. Although both the adult birds participate in the incubation of the eggs — which takes 18 days —, the female spends longer on them. The young usually leave the 'nest' only 2—4 days after they are hatched and hide in its immediate vicinity. They develop very slowly, probably because the Nightjar hunts only after dusk. They are fledged at about 16—18 days, but are not independent until they are 31—34 days old. Until then, they are cared for by the parent birds, which feed them for a long time by placing food directly in their beaks.

The Swift
(Apus apus)

Dimensions of the eggs (in mm):
Mean   — 24.9 × 16
Maximum — 28 × 17.6
Minima   — 22 × 16.2 and 22.5 × 14.3

The Swift spends most of its life on the wing and never comes down to earth voluntarily. It evidently originally inhabited rock formations and holes in tall trees. Today it lives and nests in small colonies in high, man-made structures such as towers, castles, steeples and even ordinary houses. At high altitudes it will nest in artificial nesting boxes as well as in trees.

The Swift returns from South Africa to its nesting places at the end of April and the beginning of May. It uses the same nest for several years. If the hole is occupied by other birds, it simply throws them out, together with their nest and eggs. It nests only once a year, from the middle of May to the middle of June. The flat nest consists of a collection of blades of grass, hair, wool, feathers and dry leaves blown into the air by the wind and snapped up by the bird while flying. The fine material lining the nest is bound with the Swift's saliva, which dries on contact with the air. The nest is usually 8—15 cm across (according to the shape of the base) and 1—2 cm high, with a shallow well. It takes 10—12 days to build and it is still not known for certain whether both partners participate in its construction. Nests employed for several years are naturally considerably higher than new ones.

The clutch comprises two, or sometimes three, eggs which are incubated for 18—21 days by both the parent birds. They are long, oval, white and dull. The parents both feed the young with special gobbets containing small insects caught in the air and stuck together with saliva. The young remain in the nest for an average of 42 days, but once they have left it, they never return.

126

The Kingfisher
(*Alcedo atthis*)

Dimensions of the eggs (in mm):
Mean — 22.6 × 18.8
Maxima — 22.5 × 19.4 and 22.8 × 20
Minima — 21.1 × 18.6 and 23 × 16.7

Since the main constituent of the Kingfisher's diet is small fish, it lives near water and seldom roams away. It chiefly frequents the clear running water of streams and rivers and the stagnant water of lakes and ponds, but always near the river or stream which flows into them. It nests in steep sandy or clayey banks in which it scratches out a burrow. The presence of trees or shrubs is essential, however. In mountainous regions the Kingfisher can be found at altitudes of up to 2,000 m.

The two birds need several days or a few weeks to excavate their horizontal or gently rising burrow, according to the hardness of the substrate. They dig with their beaks and throw the soil out with their short legs. The length of the burrow varies from 20 to 100 cm and the entrance is 4—6 cm across. The passage terminates in a nest chamber 12—23 cm long, 11—20 cm wide and 9—14 cm high, where the female lays five to seven eggs from the beginning of April.

Kingfishers normally nest twice, and sometimes even three times, a year. The rounded, pure white eggs lie on the bare floor of the chamber, or on food remains (such as fish-bones) left behind from the previous nesting, as the same burrow is sometimes used several times. The parent birds both sit on the eggs, which take 18—21 days to hatch. The young are fed on fish. From the differences in the size of the young we can conclude that incubation starts as soon as the first egg has been laid. The young leave the burrow after 23—27 days. Meanwhile, the female may have already started to sit on a second or third clutch in another burrow next door.

The Green Woodpecker
(Picus viridis)

Dimensions of the eggs (in mm):
Mean   — 30.9 × 22.9
Maxima   — 35.3 × 23.3 and 31.4 × 25.3
Minimum — 27 × 20

The Green Woodpecker is one of the most familiar members of this group. As a typical tree-nesting bird, it is to be found wherever there are sufficient trees, especially old ones with over-grown trunks. It can be seen mainly in open country in which small woods alternate with fields and meadows and it often inhabits old parks and gardens and avenues. In general, it can be said to prefer deciduous trees to conifers. It also prefers moderate altitudes, but here and there it can be encountered in the mountains up to 1,500 metres above sea level.

The Green Woodpecker nests in tree holes. Although capable of hacking out a nest hole for itself, it likes to use ready-made holes excavated by other woodpeckers. If a couple decides to form its own hole, the work takes about 28 days. The male always makes the first start, before pairing, and is afterwards joined by the female. Pairing and building is invariably accom-panied by typical loud calls. The hole is usually in a deciduous tree and the opening can be 1.5—10 m above the ground. Nesting takes place in April and May. The female lays five to seven glossy eggs which are white like those of all woodpeckers.

The eggs are incubated for 14—19 days and the parents take turns to sit on them and also to feed the young. The young leave the nest at the age of 15—28 days and are then fed for a further 3 weeks by the parents. While still in the nest, the young continuously utter curious wheedling cries and thereby draw attention to the position of the nest.

The Great Spotted Woodpecker
(Dendrocopos major)

Dimensions of the eggs (in mm):
Mean   — 25.3×19
Maxima — 29×19.6 and 27×21.9
Minimum — 18.7×15.1

The Great Spotted Woodpecker is undoubtedly the commonest member of this group. It occurs in all types of woods and at all altitudes right up to the upper limit of the forest belt, although it prefers mixed forests. Sometimes it will nest in large parks and old gardens. The territory of the Great Spotted Woodpecker has an area of 400,000—600,000 sq m. When not nesting, it is an extremely solitary bird, although during the winter it may join flocks of tits. It nests in the same spot several years in succession.

In its nesting preserve, the Great Spotted Woodpecker hacks out numerous holes in the trees, which may be used either for nesting or only for sleeping in, but most of which are never employed at all. Sometimes it uses other woodpecker holes, or even nesting boxes. Excavation of the nest hole takes the birds about 3 weeks and they may use it for several years. The entrance is 5—5.5 cm in diameter and the cavity is 20—30 cm deep and about 15 cm wide. The inner walls are very smooth. The height at which the hole is situated varies, ranging mainly from 4 to 10 cm; in extreme cases the entrance may be over 1 m above the ground.

The Great Spotted Woodpecker nests only once a year and lays its eggs in April or May. The four to seven white, glossy eggs usually lie on the floor of the hole without any other underlay than sawdust and shavings. During the 12—13 days' incubation period the parents take turns to sit on them and also keep the young covered for 12 days. The young constantly utter begging calls. At the age of 20—24 days they leave the hole but are trained by the parents for a further 8—14 days and return to the hole at night.

The Skylark
(Alauda arvensis)

Dimensions of the eggs (in mm):
Mean — *23.7 × 17*
Maxima — *26.6 × 17.3 and 25.6 × 18.5*
Minima — *21.1 × 16.7 and 25.1 × 15.3*

The Skylark is to be found mainly in low cornfields, clover and lucerne fields, and pastures and meadows. Sometimes, although less frequently, it will nest in mountain pastures and meadows, often high above the limits of the forest belt. In the Himalayas it inhabits table-land up to an altitude of 4,400 m. It is seldom encountered in large forest clearings.

The nest is often in a relatively deep natural hollow in the ground, situated between lumps of soil or turf in old cattle tracks, although the bird may make a shallow hollow for the nest itself. The male chooses the site for the nest. The nest is built by the female, while the male demarcates its territory in melodious song. The nest is made of dry blades of grass, small roots and leaves. At the base it is about 2 cm thick, but it thins out at the sides. The well is 8—9 cm across and about 5 cm deep.

From the middle of April the female lays three to five (very occasionally six to seven) creamy or greyish-white eggs with variable markings. The dark grey or brown spots are often so thick that they completely hide the ground colour. At the blunt end of the egg they usually form a dense ring. Clutches of light brown, reddish or white eggs are also known. The Skylark nests a second time in June. The young are hatched in 11—14 days and are fed by both parents. As a rule, they sit in the nest with their heads to one side. They leave the nest at 9 days, but are not completely independent and fully fledged until they are 3 weeks old.

The Swallow
(Hirundo rustica)

Dimensions of the eggs (in mm):
Mean   — *19.3 × 13.6*
Maxima   — *23 × 15 and 18 × 15.1*
Minimum   — *15.5 × 12*

The Swallow is actually the only bird which regularly inhabits buildings. It avoids large towns, but solitary nests and small colonies are to be found in villages and on isolated cottages. The basin type nest is open from above and is shaped like a quarter sphere. It is usually built on a base, such as a lamp-shade, a board, a small beam, electric wiring or a water-pipe in a passage, on a staircase or in a hall, but preferably in a cowshed or a stable. It is very rare to find a swallow's nest on the outside of a building.

Swallows generally start to build in the second half of April. The nest is built by both members of the pair and is made of small lumps of wet soil, clay or loam, mixed with short blades of grass and hair. It is reinforced with the birds' saliva, which dries in the air. The nest is 8—14 cm in diameter and 8 cm high and the well, which is lined with feathers, hair and blades of grass, is 7—10 cm across. The walls of the nest are 1—2 cm thick. The work of constructing it takes roughly 8 days.

The first eggs may be laid at the end of April, but usually appear in May. The breeding period extends to July, as Swallows nest twice, and sometimes three times, a year. The clutch generally comprises four to six white eggs speckled with violet-grey deep spots and brownish-red and grey surface spots. The female incubates the eggs for 16 days and the young are fed by both parents for 20—24 days. The excreta of the young are not covered with a sufficiently strong film for the adult birds to be able to remove them, with the result that they gradually pile up round the edge of the nest. Even after leaving the nest, the young are still fed by the parents, both while perching and during flight. For the first few days they return to the nest to sleep.

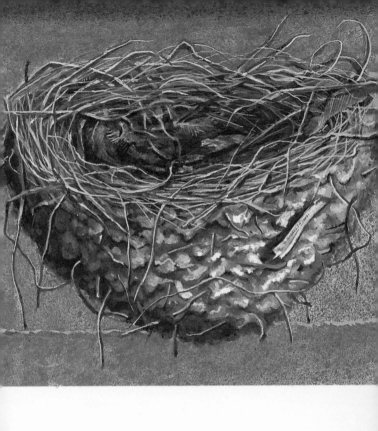

The House Martin
(Delichon urbica)

Dimensions of the eggs (in mm):
Mean   — 18.8 × 13.2
Maxima — 23.6 × 13 and 21.5 × 14.7
Minima — 16.7 × 13.1 and 19.7 × 12

Like the Swallow, the House Martin is bound to human habitations, but it originally nested in rocks and is occasionally still to be found there. It nests in isolated cottages and in villages but, unlike the Swallow, it can also be found in the centre of large towns. Another difference is that the House Martin builds its nest on the outside of buildings and only very rarely inside. Here and there we may find its nests under bridges or at the entrance to tunnels. The House Martin is a typical colony former. Its nest is always sheltered by some overhanging object, such as the eaves or ornamental facade of a house.

House Martins usually start to build their nests, or adapt old ones, at the beginning of May. A new nest, which is built by both partners, takes 8—18 days to make. The time partly depends on the weather, as wet mud is the main nest material and fewer grass blades are used than in a Swallow's nest. Such a nest, which is literally stuck on to the wall, will last for several years. The outer diameter of the nest is 11—15 cm and its height 7—12 cm. It is lined with blades of grass and feathers and the entrance is about 4 cm across.

The first clutch is laid in May and the last one may not appear until August. Two clutches are the general rule. The clutch contains four or five pure white, glossy eggs. They are incubated by both the parent birds for 12—14 days (according to the latest data 17—20 days), incubation starting when the second or third egg has been laid. The young, which are fed by both the adult birds, remain in the nest for 20—23 days. After leaving it, only a few of the young in the colony return to the nest to sleep, while the rest disperse. The adult birds return to the same nest the following year.

The Sand Martin
(Riparia riparia)

Dimensions of the eggs (in mm):
Mean — 17.3 × 12.5
Maxima — 19.9 × 12.7 and 17.7 × 13.9
Minima — 15.2 × 11.7 and 17.8 × 10.2

Few songbirds nest in burrows as the Sand Martin does. This bird is restricted in its choice of nesting sites, as it requires steep walls of soft material in which it can easily excavate a burrow. This is probably why it nests in colonies, which may comprise several hundred couples. Sand- and clay-pits and natural ravines are the most suitable places, but the Sand Martin also often nests in river banks and beside lakes and ponds.

The average depth of the burrow is 60 cm (the record is 195 cm). It is elliptical in section and is 4—6 cm wide. After first running horizontally, it slopes gently upwards and terminates in a chamber 8—12 cm high and 10—14 cm wide. The chamber contains the nest, which is a low heap of grass blades, hairs and small roots, lined with fine feathers and hair. The burrow and nest are built by both partners, although other birds can also participate in the making of the burrow.

The females generally start to lay from the middle of May. They nest twice a year. The complete clutch contains five or six eggs, which, like those of most hole-nesters, are white. They are incubated by both the parent birds for 12—16 days. For the first few days after they are hatched, the young are tended by only one of the parents, but from the fourth day they are usually fed by both. It is interesting to note that the parents do not spend the night in the burrow, but simply cover the young with feathers from the lining of the nest. Young Sand Martins leave the nest relatively soon, but they remain in the burrow and wait near the entrance for the parents to bring food. At 16—22 days they leave the burrow and never return.

The Carrion Crow
(Corvus corone)

Dimensions of the eggs (in mm):
Mean   — 41.7 × 29.5
Maxima — 49.7 × 32.3 and 41.1 × 34
Minima — 36.4 × 28.3 and 42.7 × 26.5

Carrion Crows like a varied terrain in which open country alternates with small woods, copses or groups of trees. In some parts of Europe they nest near human habitations, in parks, cemeteries and lanes. In woods, they always nest near the periphery. In isolated cases they have been known to nest on the ground, on tall buildings or on electric pylons.

Crows build their nests early in the spring, before the trees start to bud. The nest is situated high up in a tree, either on a forked branch or beside the trunk. It is a large, compact structure about 60 cm in diameter, built on a foundation of thick, dry branches intermingled with turf, grass blades and parts of other plants. The well, which is only 10 cm deep, is lined with finer material, such as hair, moss and dry grass. Both the partners participate in the construction of the nest, but their tasks are somewhat divided. The male fetches most of the material (it does not collect the dry branches from the ground, but snaps them off), while the female does the actual building.

The first clutches appear at the end of March and in April. There is usually only one a year, not counting substitute clutches. The female starts to brood as soon as the first egg has been laid and the male keeps it conscientiously supplied with food. The four or five bluish-green eggs are speckled with greenish-grey, olive-green and blackish-brown spots and dots. They are incubated for 17—18 days. The young remain in the nest for 31—32 days. During the first week the female keeps them covered the whole 24 hours, but later only at night. They are very quiet, and since the adult birds are also very cautious, the nest is difficult to find.

The Rook
(Corvus frugilegus)

Dimensions of the eggs (in mm):
Mean — *40 × 28*
Maxima — *47.4 × 30 and 42 × 32*
Minima — *32.4 × 26.3 and 33.4 × 25.5*

In general, Rooks can be said to be lowland birds. They prefer cultivated country, with large fields and meadows where they can find food, and with at least a few groups of tall trees suitable for accommodating their colonies, which sometimes comprise several hundred nests. The Rook is becoming increasingly associated with human communities and today it is not uncommon to find small colonies in the middle of cities, in parks or cemeteries, on isolated large trees and sometimes even on big buildings. There is room for up to ten to fifteen nests in the top of a large, old tree. Solitary nesting is not common among Rooks.

The Rook's nest is not so strong as that of the Carrion Crow, but it is usually larger, as Rooks like to use old nests, which they simply adapt. Both partners participate in the work, but the male generally only fetches the material. The foundations consist of large branches, while the top is made of moss, turf and mud. The relatively small well is lined with grass, leaves and hair. The female starts to lay in the second half of March and the clutch contains three to five eggs. The eggs are similarly coloured to those of the Carrion Crow, but the ground colour is lighter and the spots are duller. They are incubated for 16—18 days by the female, which the male keeps supplied with food. The female keeps the newly hatched young covered for 10 days, during which the male feeds the whole family. The screeching young remain in the nest for 4—5 weeks. During the sixth week they perch round the nest and then leave it. Rooks nest once a year.

144

The Jackdaw
(*Corvus monedula*)

Dimensions of the eggs (in mm):
Mean   —   35.7 × 25.4
Maxima   —   39.8 × 25.9 and 32.5 × 27.5
Minimum —   29.3 × 21

It is difficult to define the ecological requirements of this active and sociable bird, which occurs wherever it can find convenient nest holes and niches. Since it finds its food in open country, it avoids large, coherent forests. In suitable places it forms colonies. Originally it inhabited rock formations and old, hollow trees, but today it also frequently settles on tall buildings, ruins and holes in the walls of sand- and clay-pits, and even occupies natural and self-excavated burrows. If unable to find a hole, it will use the nests of other birds, or build its own nest in a tree. The nest varies in size according to the circumstances and consists of a heap of dry branches, grass, turf and mud intermingled with finer material. The well is lined with feathers, hair and fine vegetable material.

Laying takes place in April and May and the clutch consists of five or six light greenish-blue or greenish-grey eggs thinly speckled with grey of greyish-brown spots, which are often denser at the blunt end. The Jackdaw nests only once a year, but if the clutch is lost, a fresh one is laid. The female evidently does not start to incubate the eggs until just before laying the last one. It is still not absolutely certain whether only the female sits on the eggs, or whether the parents take turns, but whichever it is, the female plays the major role. The incubation period is 16—19 days. The young are fed in the nest for about a month and are fledged at 5 weeks. The parents bring them food in a special sac in their throat and continue to feed them for a short time after they have learnt to fly.

The Magpie
(Pica pica)

Dimensions of the eggs (in mm):
Mean — *34.8 × 24.7*
Maxima — *40.2 × 26.2 and 37.5 × 28*
Minima — *27.7 × 24 and 33.7 × 21.2*

The Magpie is a typical inhabitant of cultivated country at low and moderate altitudes, characterized by alternation of fields with woods, thickets and groups of trees. It nests in trees and bushes, sometimes at the height of a man, but usually high enough to allow a clear view of its surroundings. As a result, it prefers tall trees and bushes. It seldom nests in large woods.

The nest is roofed over with a characteristic open-work arch of foliage and the entrance is at the side. The foundations consist mainly of branches and are surmounted by a layer of mud and turf. The well is lined with small roots, leaves, blades of grass and hair. As a rule, Magpies build a new nest every year, but not infrequently they simply refurbish an old one.

The five to seven (in exceptional cases up to ten) eggs are occasionally laid at the end of March, but generally in April or May. They are greenish, brownish or light blue and are speckled with brown spots and dots, which are thicker at the blunt end. The Magpie nests once a year, but if the first clutch is lost, a substitute one is laid. The eggs are incubated for 17—18 days by the female, although the male has also been known to share in this task. Since the female starts to brood when the first eggs are laid, the young are of varying sizes. They remain in the nest for 22—24 days. After leaving it, they often draw attention to their position by their feeding-time calls. The family remains intact for some time after the young have left the nest.

The Jay
(*Garrulus glandarius*)

Dimensions of the eggs (in mm):
Mean   —   30.6 × 22.6
Maxima —   34.5 × 26.2 and 34 × 24.6
Minima —   27.8 × 22.7 and 32.1 × 21.1

No walk through the woods would be complete without hearing the chattering call of the Jay. During the nesting period we can encounter this bird in all types of forests — in lowland deciduous woods and in mixed and purely coniferous woods at moderate and high altitudes, as far as the upper limit of the forest belt. The Jay nests 2—6 m above the ground, in trees and tall bushes. The nest is built by both the partners about 3 weeks before the eggs are laid. It is rather small compared with the nests of other birds of the crow family, as it is only about 30 cm across; it is flat, with a relatively deep well. Thin twigs form the main building material, the inner wall is faced with grass and the well is lined with small roots and hairs. The outset of laying seems to depend on when the trees put forth their leaves, and usually comes in April or May. The clutch contains five to seven (in exceptional cases up to ten) eggs.

The glossy oval eggs are greyish-green or olive-green, with fine brownish-red or brown speckles. At the blunt end there are sometimes fine, filamentous black lines. The parents both take turns to sit on the eggs and the incubation period is 16—17 days. According to the available literature, the female starts to brood after laying the first or second egg, but despite this the young are the same size. The young do not make much noise while in the nest. At about 3 weeks they leave the nest, but the adult birds continue to feed them and the family remains united right into the autumn.

The Great Tit
(Parus major)

Dimensions of the eggs (in mm):
Mean   — 17.2 × 13.4
Maxima — 20.5 × 13.4 and 17.8 × 14.7
Minima — 15.1 × 13.2 and 15.8 × 12.1

The Great Tit is a modest bird, which occurs wherever it finds trees. It nests at all altitudes, from the lowlands to the upper limits of the forest belt, and in all types of woods — deciduous, mixed and coniferous — and is not afraid of the presence of man. Its favourite nest sites are tree-holes, but in an emergency it will make do with a hole in a wall, a fissure in a rock or the abandoned nest of some larger bird, which it uses as the foundations for its own. It also has a predilection for nesting boxes.

The nest, which is built entirely by the female, is made of moss, rootlets, grass and lichens and is lined with fine hair, animal fluff and feathers. The female also chooses the site, while the male merely acts as a guide. Sometimes the nest is a really large structure completely filling the hole. The well is 7—8 cm across and 3—4 cm deep.

The Great Tit nests in April or May and again in June or July. The relatively large clutches contain eight to twelve (in extreme cases up to eighteen) eggs. The white eggs are speckled with more or less brick-red surface spots and sometimes have mauvish-grey deep spots. They are incubated solely by the female, which generally does not start to brood until just before the clutch is complete. Like other tits, it covers the eggs with nest material on leaving them. The incubation period is 13—14 days. Both the adult birds feed the young. They do so very assiduously and on the last day before the young leave the nest they make up to 800 journeys for food. The young remain in the nest for 15—21 days.

The Coal Tit
(Parus ater)

Dimensions of the eggs (in mm):
Mean — *14.8 × 11.6*
Maxima — *16.5 × 12.3 and 14.2 × 12.6*
Minima — *13.1 × 10.9 and 13.4 × 10.5*

The Coal Tit prefers to live in coniferous forests, but will make do with mixed woods if they contain at least groups of conifers. It is equally content with spruce, silver fir and pine forests, but avoids pure larch growths. It nests at all altitudes, right to the upper limit of the forest belt.

Like the Great Tit, it nests in holes, though not too far above the ground. It prefers tree-holes, but as these are somewhat rare in timber monocultures, it often nests between the roots of trees, in cracks and holes in the ground and sometimes among stones, in fissures in rocks, or even in abandoned mouse or mole holes. It also gratefully accepts nesting boxes. The size of the nest depends on the roominess of the hole. It is built by both partners, is made of similar material to that of the Great Tit and is richly lined, except that fewer feathers are used.

The Coal Tit always nests twice (in exceptional cases three times) a year, between April and June, and the clutch contains an average of eight eggs (maximum twelve). The eggs are white and are regularly speckled with small rusty-brown spots and blotches, which sometimes form a ring at the blunt end. The female starts to brood just before the last one is laid and the young are hatched in 14—17 days. They remain in the nest hole for 16—23 days and are fed by both the adult birds, which continue to care for them for a short time after they are fledged.

The Long-tailed Tit
(*Aegithalos caudatus*)

Dimensions of the eggs (in mm):
Mean   — *13.9×11.2*
Maxima — *16.4×11.2 and 15×12*
Minima — *13×10.9 and 13.8×10.1*

This small and lively bird frequents mixed and deciduous forests with thick undergrowth and old, overgrown gardens and parks during the nesting season. Few of our native birds can vie with it as builders.

The nest is large compared with the size of the bird. It resembles a bag, as it has a wide base and narrows towards the top. The entrance, which is in the upper third, is 2—4 cm wide. It is a complicated structure, which takes both the birds 9—18 days to build. The actual building is done by the female, while the male fetches the material. The thick walls are made of moss, bast, fine bark (especially birch), lichen, hair, cobwebs and cocoon silk. Inside it is thickly lined with feathers, wool and hair. It is about 25 cm high and 10 cm wide and when dry weighs 40 g. It is placed in a sheltered, shady spot beside the trunk of a small tree or in a fork in a bush, 1—3 m above the ground.

The first clutches, which contain ten to twelve eggs, appear in April and May and the second ones, comprising six to seven eggs, in May and June. The dull, yellowish-white or greyish-white eggs are marked with red spots. The spots are sometimes indistinct, so that the eggs appear to be plainly coloured. The female starts to incubate them just before laying, or while actually laying, the last one. It is not known with certainty whether the male participates in the incubation of the eggs, which takes 12—13 days. The young remain in the nest for 14 days. They are sometimes fed by unpaired, unrelated Long-tailed Tits, as well as by their own parents. The second batch of young is often fed by the first batch.

The Short-toed Treecreeper
(Certhia brachydactyla)

Dimensions of the eggs (in mm):
Mean — *16.1×12.1*
Maxima — *17.2×11.8 and 16.5×12.4*
Minima — *14.1×11.5 and 16.6×11.2*

The Short-toed Treecreeper occurs more in deciduous woods and since it lives on insects, which it looks for behind bark, it chooses tall, old trees with cracked, rough bark. It lives at low and moderate altitudes and is never found high up in the mountains. As well as in woods, it is to be found in avenues, groups of trees, parks and cemeteries.

The nest is usually placed behind cracked and peeling bark, or in a crevice or a small hole in a tree, behind boards and beams in wooden buildings, in woodpiles, etc. Its shape is always adapted to its location. It is generally 10—16 cm high, but if built on a horizontal base it can also be flat, although as a rule it has compressed sides. It is an untidy pile of dry twigs, grass, bast and cocoon silk. The well has a soft feather lining. The nest is usually situated 2 m above the ground but in some cases it may be higher.

The Short-toed Treecreeper probably breeds only once a year, in May or June. The female lays six or seven, but occasionally up to twelve, milky-white eggs with bright red surface spots and mauvish-grey deep spots. It incubates the eggs alone and is fed by the male. The incubation period is 15 days. The young take about 16 days to rear and again the female has most of the responsibility. There is still some uncertainty about the nest biology of this bird. We can sometimes find young still being fed in the nest in July, indicating that the Short-toed Treecreeper may also breed twice in a year.

The Nuthatch
(*Sitta europaea*)

Dimensions of the eggs (in mm):
Mean   — 19.4 × 14.8
Maxima — 21.4 × 14 and 20 × 16
Minima — 16.5 × 13.5 and 19.1 × 13.2

The Nuthatch always inhabits woods with tall trees. It nests primarily in deciduous and mixed woods. It is also quite common in parks, overgrown gardens, cemeteries and avenues. Early in the spring the male stakes its claim to a territory. It remains there the whole year and defends the area stubbornly against all intruders.

The Nuthatch generally nests in old woodpecker holes. As the openings of these holes are too wide for it, the female daubs the entrance with mud to make it narrower. This task may take as long as 14 days and much of the work is useless. For example, the bird may also daub the space above the entrance to the hole, or prolong the entrance into a kind of tube. Such 'extensions' can weigh as much as 0.75 kg.

As a rule, the female builds the nest while still walling up the entrance. It is not a nest in the true meaning of the word, but is a loose litter of fragments of bark, leaves and bast. Pine bark is particularly popular.

Between May and June the female lays six to eight milky-white eggs with indistinct, grey and greyish-mauve deep spots and rusty-red surface spots, which are sometimes thicker at the blunt end. The female starts to sit on the eggs after the last or penultimate one has been laid and, except for short breaks, stays on them until the young are hatched, i.e. 15—18 days. Both the parent birds feed the young in the nest for a comparatively long period — 23—24 days. The young leave the hole fully fledged, but the parents look after them for a further 8—10 days until they are completely independent.

The Wren
(Troglodytes troglodytes)

Dimensions of the eggs (in mm):
Mean   — 16.5 × 12.5
Maxima — 18.9 × 13.2 and 18.3 × 14
Minima — 15.1 × 12.6 and 16.1 × 12

The Wren — second smallest of our native birds — always lives in shady, mixed, deciduous and sometimes coniferous woods with dense undergrowth, in the lowlands and high up in the mountains. The male chooses the nesting area and starts to build several nests — sometimes as many as eight — at once. The nests are placed under fallen trees, between tree roots, below eroded banks, under bridges, in holes in old walls, in winter feeding-troughs for game, in tangled thickets or in hedges. Not infrequently it will pull old nests to pieces and use the material to make new ones. None of these nests has a lining, however. The male must first of all court a female, which inspects the display of nests and then lines one of them with wool, hair and feathers as a breeding nest. The rest are left as play nests, in which the male, and later on the whole family, spends the night.

The Wren's nest is a large spherical structure made of moss and lichens and occasionally of stems and leaves. The opening is at the side, about half-way up the nest. The nest is about 9—12 cm across and up to 16 cm high. Its shape conforms to that of the cavity in which it is usually situated. It is placed close to the ground and is always carefully concealed.

The Wren nests twice a year, between April and July, and the clutch contains an average of six (five to ten) white eggs speckled with small rust-coloured spots. In extreme cases they may be unspeckled. The female incubates the eggs for 16—18 days and starts to brood some time after laying the third egg. The young leave the nest at the age of 14—20 days. For a short time the family remains united and spends the night in the play nests.

The Mistle Thrush
(Turdus viscivorus)

Dimensions of the eggs (in mm):
Mean   — *29.5 × 22.2*
Maxima — *35.8 × 22.7 and 30.6 × 24.4*
Minima — *26.9 × 22 and 28 × 19.6*

The Mistle Thrush is the largest of the European thrushes. During the nesting season it mainly inhabits coniferous forests and to a lesser degree mixed forests. In Western Europe, however, it commonly nests in deciduous woods and even in parks and orchards. It occurs at both low and high altitudes. The nest is built in trees, comparatively high (1.5—15 m) above the ground, a favourite site being the fork of a large branch, often near the trunk.

The nest of the Mistle Thrush is relatively large compared with the nests of other thrushes. It has quite a wide base and is very untidy in appearance. Twigs, small roots and blades of grass are used as the building materials. The walls are reinforced with soil and mud, and moss and lichen are often added to the surface. The well is lined with dry grass stalks. The whole nest is up to 25 cm across and about 12 cm high and the well is 11 cm across and 5 cm deep. It is built by the female in about 8 days.

The Mistle Thrush nests twice a year, between the end of March and June. The female lays four or five eggs and incubates them unaided for 12—16 days. The eggs are generally light bluish-green or brownish-cream and are covered with reddish-brown surface spots and mauvish-grey deep spots. They are more gaily coloured than the eggs of other thrushes. The parent birds both feed the young for 14—16 days. The data of different observers on the part played by the male in feeding and also in the incubation of the eggs vary, however. Young Mistle Thrushes leave the nest before they are fully fledged and remain in the near-by branches. They are not able to fly until they are 20 days old.

The Song Thrush
(Turdus philomelos)

Dimensions of the eggs (in mm):
Mean   —   *27.3 × 20.4*
Maxima   —   *31.2 × 20.9 and 28 × 23*
Minima   —   *24.7 × 20.2 and 27 × 19.2*

No wood would be complete without the Song Thrush. It mainly frequents coniferous forests, is quite common in mixed woods, but is rarer in purely deciduous woods. It is to be found at all altitudes, right up to the limit of the forest belt. In recent times it has also started to settle in town parks and gardens and has thus joined the blackbird in this respect.

The nest is built in dense vegetation, which means that the Song Thrush avoids forests without undergrowth. It is usually placed at the foot of large conifers, but sometimes in shrubs or on deciduous trees providing good cover. The usual height for the nest is 1—3 m, but seldom more, above the ground. In towns the Song Thrush may also nest on buildings. The nest is made of twigs, blades of grass and dry grass, with an admixture of moss and lichen, but unlike the nests of other thrushes, the deep, basin-shaped well is lined with a special paste obtained by mixing wood mould, soil and saliva, which dries to form a smooth, hard wall. The dimensions of the nest are as follows: total diameter 10—18 cm, diameter of well 9—11 cm, depth of well 6—7.5 cm, height of nest 8—9.5 cm. The first nesting period is from April to May and the second from June to July. The clutch usually consists of five (four to six) light blue eggs speckled with black or blackish-brown spots. As well as building the nest, the female has sole responsibility for the incubation of the eggs. It starts to brood when the last egg is laid and sits on the clutch for a total of 12—13 days. The young are fed by both parent birds and leave the nest in 12—14 days, before they are fully fledged.

The Blackbird
(Turdus merula)

Dimensions of the eggs (in mm):
Mean — *29.5 × 21.5*
Maxima — *35 × 21.5* and *34 × 24*
Minimum — *24.2 × 19*

Like the Song Thrush, the Blackbird has gradually become a town-dweller, evidently because it found more food in man's vicinity. It has not disappeared entirely from the woods, however, and in Eastern Europe it has not yet taken to living in towns. We thus have forest and urban Blackbird populations, each with its own nest biology, determined by the different conditions. Forest-dwelling Blackbirds are not fussy in their choice of environment, but do not like woods which are too dry or too light. They are to be found in the lowlands and high up in the mountains.

The nesting site is selected by common choice. These birds originally nested only in trees with thick foliage and in bushes, but they now nest almost anywhere.

Urban Blackbirds have a wide variety of nesting sites. They may nest in piles of twigs and wood in hedges, under roofs, on cornices, behind gutter-pipes, in short, anywhere where they can find a base and shelter for the nest. The nest is made of twigs, leaves and moss bound with saliva and the well is lined with fine dry blades of grass and leaves and sometimes with feathers. Its total diameter is 13—20 cm, its height 7—9 cm; the diameter of the well is 7—10 cm and the depth of the well 4—6 cm.

The Blackbird nests two or three times a year. The first clutches usually appear in April — in the case of town-dwelling birds in March. They contain four to six eggs, while the average number in the second and third clutch is four. The eggs are light green or greenish-blue, with rusty-red spots, which are sometimes thicker at the blunt end and in other cases may be blurred. The female incubates the eggs for 12—14 days, occasionally relieved by the male. The young are fed by both the parent birds for the 2 weeks they are in the nest and for a further 2 weeks after they are fledged.

The Wheatear
(Oenanthe oenanthe)

Dimensions of the eggs (in mm):
Mean — 20.8 × 15.6
Maxima — 24.8 × 15.4 and 23.4 × 17.5
Minima — 18.6 × 15.7 and 22 × 14.1

The Wheatear inhabits flat, open country at all altitudes. In Europe it is found on the coast and high up in the mountains (2,500 m). Originally it lived in dry waste-land, steppes and dry, sandy regions, among falls of rock and on stony mountain sides. In the plains of North Germany it also lives in wide forest clearings.

The nest is always built in a hole or a niche — between stones, in rock fissures, in holes in the walls of sand- and clay-pits and sometimes in the burrows of mammals and birds — and always on or close to the ground. It is seldom to be found in a tree hole. The nest is an untidy structure made of blades of grass, leaves, small roots and twigs, and conifer needles and is about 12 cm in diameter. The well is about 7 cm across and only 3.5 cm deep. It is thickly lined with feathers, plant fibres, fur and horsehair. The pair chooses the territory soon after their arrival and shortly afterwards the male starts to stake its claim in song and to defend its domain against intruders. It is not yet clear whether both birds build the nest, or only the female, but the latter certainly does most of the work. It builds mainly in the morning and late afternoon.

The five or six (occasionally seven) eggs are incubated for 13—14 days, solely by the female. The parent birds both feed the young for about 15 days, until they leave the nest. The young are able to fly at 19 days, but when in danger they often hide among stones. In Central Europe the Wheatear nests only once a year, from the second half of May to July. Under adverse conditions, or if the clutch is lost, it nests a second time. The single-coloured, light blue eggs are smooth and have a faint gloss.

The Whinchat
(*Saxicola rubetra*)

Dimensions of the eggs (in mm):
Mean — *18.7 × 14.4*
Maxima — *21.5 × 14.5 and 19.8 × 15.5*
Minima — *16.6 × 13.8 and 19.3 × 13.5*

The Whinchat inhabits wet meadows and pastures overgrown with tall vegetation. It also nests in large forest clearings and, in Western Europe, in fields. The female always chooses the site for the nest and builds it unaided. It sometimes does so at the end of March, but usually in April. It is extremely difficult to find the Whinchat's nest in the thick vegetation, as it is sunk in the ground and is always well concealed by the surrounding plants or the branches of a bush.

The relatively tidy nest is woven from dry blades of grass, leaves and small roots and is lined with plants, fluff and horsehair, but seldom with feathers. The female lays the five to six bluish-green eggs in the second half of May or in June. There is usually only one clutch a year. The female starts to sit on the eggs on laying the last or penultimate one. The incubation period is 13 days. According to most of the data in the available literature, only the female incubates the eggs, but exceptions have been known. The male sometimes feeds the brooding female.

The bluish-green eggs are generally plainly coloured, but are sometimes very finely speckled with rusty-brown spots. As soon as the young are hatched, the male also starts to care for them assiduously. Like most small, ground-nesting songbirds, young Whinchats disperse from the nest relatively soon and hide near-by. They leave the nest at 12—13 days and are fed by the parents for a further 2—3 weeks. When 17—19 days old they start to fly.

The Redstart
(Phoenicurus phoenicurus)

Dimensions of the eggs (in mm):
Mean   — 18.8 × 13.7
Maxima — 20.7 × 13.5 and 18.8 × 15.1
Minima — 16.1 × 13.1 and 16.6 × 12.6

The Redstart, being a typical tree-dwelling bird, settles wherever it finds an adequate number of tall trees. It can be found at low and moderate altitudes and in deciduous, mixed and pine woods, but less often in fir woods. It is often seen in old parks and gardens, although it can also be found among jagged rocks and even on mountains, if the trees are sufficiently tall.

The Redstart generally hides its nest in holes in old trees, in empty woodpecker holes, or in niches left by broken branches, etc. It also accepts nesting boxes. Sometimes it will nest in a hole in a wall or a crack in a rock and, although nesting in ground holes is a rare occurrence in Central Europe, the Redstart quite commonly nests in the ground in the pine woods of Northern Europe.

The nest, which is situated 1—5 m above the ground, is built entirely by the female. It is made of blades of grass, moss, small roots and leaves and is thickly lined with feathers and hair. The clutch of six or seven (in exceptional cases eight or nine) eggs sometimes does not appear in the nest for a month. The eggs are bluish-green and are only occasionally marked with indistinct, brownish-red spots.

The female starts to sit on the eggs before laying the last one and incubates them for 12—14 days — evidently without any assistance from the male. The parent birds both feed the young for 14—15 days. It was found that one pair of Redstarts fed their young 3,457 times over a 12-day period. The Redstart usually nests only once a year and it is not known how long the parents continue to feed the young after the latter have left the nest.

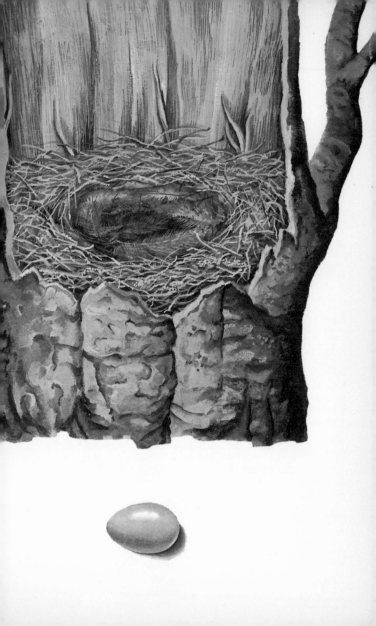

The Black Redstart
(*Phoenicurus ochruros*)

Dimensions of the eggs (in mm):
Mean — *19.3 × 14.2*
Maxima — *21.8 × 15 and 20.6 × 16.4*
Minima — *17 × 14.5 and 17.2 × 13.3*

The grating song of the Black Redstart can be heard on rocky mountain sides high above the forest belt and in lowland rock formations, in boulders at the foot of high mountains, in quarries and in rocky river valleys. These are its original home. We do not know when the first birds started to exchange rocks for houses and other buildings, but the process evidently took place long ago. Today the Black Redstart occupies both types of habitat and even seems to prefer the company of human beings.

The sites of the nests of the two populations obviously differ. The former nest in niches and cracks in the rocks, while 'civilized' birds accept any dark corner and nest in lofts, holes in walls, ruins, sheds and summer-houses, in building material stores in brickyards and elsewhere. The general shape of the nest conforms to the chosen niche and it can be either flat or high. The nest is a more or less untidy heap of dry stems and roots and the well is lined with wool and hair and sometimes with feathers. The Black Redstart nests twice a year, between April and July. The glossy eggs are usually pure white, but sometimes have a faint bluish tinge and are very occasionally speckled with small red spots. There are usually five or six in a clutch. The female builds the nest and incubates the eggs unaided. The young are hatched in 13—14 days and for 12—16 days they are fed by the parents in the nest. They leave the nest before they are fully fledged, but remain near it for a long time, tended by the parents.

The Nightingale
(Luscinia megarhynchos)

Dimensions of the eggs (in mm):
Mean — *20.9 × 15.5*
Maxima — *24 × 16.5 and 16.8 × 23*
Minima — *18.3 × 16 and 19.1 × 13.8*

The Nightingale is confined to warm lowlands and is found only in woods with sufficient shrubs and undergrowth to provide it with adequate shelter. It nests in woods, large parks and gardens, small game preserves and cemeteries. In Central Europe it occurs at altitudes of up to only 400 m, but the further south we go, the higher the altitudes at which we can find it.

The nest is built close to the ground or directly on it, in tangled branches and grass or in thick, prickly shrubs and occasionally in the branches of small conifers. It is a small, compact structure built on a base of dry leaves, with a superstructure made of small roots, blades of grass and moss and a well lined with hair and fine rootlets. It is a messy-looking affair and is built in 3 days by the female — evidently without any assistance.

As a rule, the Nightingale nests only once a year, in May or June. The clutch comprises four to six eggs, but usually five. These tend to vary in form. They are generally plain olive-brown or olive-green, but sometimes they have brown spots and delicate, black scroll markings on a light green ground. The male does not help with the incubation of the eggs, which takes 13 days. The care of the young is also left entirely to the female for the first few days, but after a time the male starts to take an interest in them and fetches food. At first, it hands the food to the female, but later on both parents busily feed the young. The young leave the nest and disperse into the surrounding vegetation before they are fully developed. They undertake short flights 3 days later and after 10 days they are independent.

The Robin
(Erithacus rubecula)

Dimensions of the eggs (in mm):
Mean — *19.4 × 14.8*
Maxima — *22.3 × 15.5 and 20.5 × 17*
Minima — *18 × 16.6 and 18.5 × 14*

The original and main abode of this lovable little bird is any kind of wood where there is undergrowth, from lowland copses to high fir woods. It is at home everywhere, although it definitely prefers young growths to tall forests. We can also encounter the Robin in large orchards and parks and in Western Europe — particularly in Britain — it is a familiar sight in towns, where it frequents parks and gardens. The nest, which is built by the female, is well concealed in a hollow in the ground, in the hole left by a fallen tree, below an overhanging bank, in a rotting stump or under a stone bridge, etc., and as a rule is on or just above the ground. In some regions the Robin nests in hedges, on buildings overgrown with creepers, and even in nesting boxes. Dry leaves, moss, blades of grass and lichen form the main building material and the nest is lined with fluff, hair and feathers. It is a somewhat untidy structure 9—10 cm in diameter and 5 cm high, while the well is about 7 cm across.

The two clutches, which are laid in April or May and in June or July, contain five to six eggs. The eggs are white and are thickly or sparsely speckled with rusty-brown surface spots and isolated mauvish-brown deep spots. As with most songbirds, they are incubated by the female for 13—14 days and the male fetches food. The young remain in the nest about 2 weeks and then, before they are fully fledged, disperse into the surrounding vegetation. The male continues to care for them, while the female sometimes starts to sit on the second clutch.

The Great Reed Warbler
(*Acrocephalus arundinaceus*)

Dimensions of the eggs (in mm):
Mean   — *22.6 × 16.3*
Maxima — *24.8 × 16.3 and 23 × 17.2*
Minima — *20.9 × 16.2 and 21.2 × 15.3*

The Great Reed Warbler is an occasional visitor to the British Isles. It is among the reed beds of East Anglia and along the south coast that it is most likely to be seen. Its large, basket-like nest, which is usually 10—12 cm across and 15—20 cm high, is placed in reeds or osiers at the sides of lakes, ponds and quiet rivers. The nest is built by the female in about 5 days, with only moral support from the male. It is cleverly suspended from between four to nine reed blades, which pass through the walls. The stems and leaves of different aquatic plants, collected on and beside the water, form the main building material. The well is lined with a thin layer of different parts of plants and moss and relatively rarely with animal and plant fluff or feathers. The edges curve slightly inwards to prevent the eggs from falling into the water, as the nest is almost always hung above the water at a height of 0.3—1.4 m from the surface. As the nest is built while the reeds are still growing, the distance between it and the water steadily increases.

The Great Reed Warbler usually nests only once a year, between May and June, but may occasionally nest twice a year. The four or five (in exceptional cases three or six) bluish-green eggs are marked with olive-brown or blackish-brown surface spots and with grey deep spots. The parent birds both incubate the eggs and in some cases the male has been observed feeding the sitting female. The young are hatched in 13—15 days and are fed for 12 days by the parents in the nest. Four days after leaving the nest they start to fly about among the rushes.

The Reed Warbler
(Acrocephalus scirpaceus)

Dimensions of the eggs (in mm):
Mean — 18.6 × 13.8
Maxima — 20.9 × 13.8 and 19.7 × 14.9
Minima — 16.5 × 13 and 17.4 × 12.6

The Reed Warbler is sometimes content with quite a small patch of rushes beside a lake, pond, pool or creek for its typical basket-like nest. The nest is built by the female, while the male encourages it in song. The thin, narrow leaves of aquatic plants form the main material and the female cleverly weaves them round the blades of three to six rushes growing close together. The well is very deep and in newly built nests the edges curve slightly inwards, so that even when the reeds sway in a high wind the eggs do not fall out. The nest is lined with fine, small leaves and sometimes with cobwebs, but only seldom with hair and feathers. The building of the nest, which takes about 5 days, is started when the reeds have attained a suitable height. The nest is 7.5—8 cm across and 5—7 cm high, and the well is 4—5 cm deep. It is suspended 20—100 cm above the water. It is not uncommon for the nest to be placed on the branches of shrubs and willows overhanging the ground.

The Reed Warbler nests once or twice a year, between May and July. The female usually lays four or five eggs, but occasionally three. The eggs are thickly marked with large, olive-brown spots on a white ground. Sometimes the spots are denser towards the blunt end of the egg and at other times they form a vague ring. The main spots are sometimes interspersed with small black dots. The parent birds both take turns to sit on the eggs. Incubation, which takes 11—12 days, evidently starts when the last egg is laid. The parent birds likewise both feed the young. Sometimes the male passes the food to the female, which feeds the young itself. After 9—13 days the young birds leave the nest. They are not yet able to fly, but can cling firmly to the reeds.

The Blackcap
(Sylvia atricapilla)

Dimensions of the eggs (in mm):
Mean   — *19.7 × 14.6*
Maxima   — *21.6 × 14.6 and 20.5 × 16.1*
Minimum — *17.1 × 13.3*

During the nesting season, this excellent vocalist lives mainly in deciduous and coniferous forests and in woods with dense undergrowth, but it is also found in mixed growths, parks, overgrown valleys and ravines. It follows the course of streams almost to the limits of the forest belt. For its nesting site it chooses a forked branch in a thick bush, the dense top of a young conifer, a tangle of large weeds or a thorn-bush. The nest is seldom more than 2 m above the ground and is rather more solidly built than that of other songbirds. It is made of stems, roots, lichen and plant fluff and we often find horsehair in the lining of the well. It is built by both the birds and is 10—11 cm in diameter. The well is about 5 cm across and 6 cm deep. The Blackcap's nest is constructed similarly to that of the Whitethroat.

The Blackcap nests twice a year, between May and July, and generally lays four or five, but occasionally six eggs. The colouring of the eggs is very variable. They are usually brownish-white or greyish, with grey deep spots and dark brown surface spots with blurred edges. These are sometimes interspersed with large, reddish-brown spots (stigmata), but even plain reddish and other spotted variants are not uncommon. The adult birds both take turns to sit on the eggs. Incubation, which takes 12—14 days, sometimes starts when the last egg is laid, but sometimes already with the second one. The young are fed for 10—11 days.

The Whitethroat
(Sylvia communis)

Dimensions of the eggs (in mm):
Mean   — *18.1 × 13.8*
Maxima — *20.8 × 14.6 and 17.5 × 15.4*
Minima — *16.1 × 13.4 and 17.2 × 12.8*

The Whitethroat inhabits thickets and open country. It nests in the most diverse types of shrubs, in hedges, at the edge of forests, on waste-land, in deserted quarries and ravines, beside streams and stagnant water and can even be found high in the mountains and in thickly overgrown forest clearings.

When the male returns from its winter quarters, it chooses a territory and builds several rough nests, one of which is later completed by the female. It uses similar material to the Blackcap, but weaves plant and animal fluff and cocoon silk into the edge of the nest. The nest is situated close to the ground, usually in the thickest part of a bush.

The Whitethroat generally nests twice a year, between May and July. The four or five eggs are somewhat variably coloured. As a rule they are greenish-grey, with grey deep spots and olivebrown surface spots, but can also be yellowish, brownish or white, with reddish spots. Both the parent birds incubate the eggs, for a period of 12—13 days. The young take 3—18 hours to free themselves from the egg. After the young are hatched, the parents sit on them continuously for the first 4—5 days and after that keep them covered at night until the ninth or tenth day. By then the young are fledged and have no further need of added warmth. The parents feed them for 3 more weeks, during which they learn to fly.

The Chiffchaff
(Phylloscopus collybita)

Dimensions of the eggs (in mm):
Mean   — 14.8 × 11.5
Maxima — 17.2 × 12.3 and 16 × 13
Minima — 13.3 × 11.5 and 14.7 × 11.3

The Chiffchaff inhabits any type of wood, from the lowlands right up to the limits of the forest belt in the mountains. Since it is a ground-nesting bird, it chooses places with undergrowth, where its nest can be adequately concealed. In tall timber it is always found in more open parts, in undergrowth or groups of young trees. Otherwise it can be encountered in large parks and old, overgrown gardens.

The first to return in the spring is the male, which chooses a territory. The female, which arrives later, selects the actual site for the nest and starts to build it, accompanied by the male. The nest is a spherical, covered-in formation hidden in a tangle of different plants, such as a clump of grass, heather or bilberry plants, on or close to the ground. It is made chiefly of old leaves and blades of grass and sometimes contains moss and lichen. The well is lined with hair, wool and a few feathers. The relatively wide entrance is a slanting opening near the top, so that if we look inside we can see the eggs.

The clutch contains five or six (in rare cases seven) eggs, which the female lays in May or June. There is a second clutch in July. The eggs are white and are speckled with light, reddish-brown surface spots and mauvish-grey deep spots, which sometimes form an indistinct ring at the blunt .end. They are incubated by the female, which starts to brood when the last one is laid. The young are hatched in 13—14 days. For a further 13—14 days the female feeds them in the nest and continues to watch over them long after they have left it.

The Wood Warbler
(Phylloscopus sibilatrix)

Dimensions of the eggs (in mm):
Mean — *15.9 × 12.4*
Maxima — *18.4 × 12.5 and 16.8 × 13.6*
Minima — *14.4 × 12.2 and 15.5 × 11.5*

There is not a beech-wood in which we do not find the Wood Warbler. We can also encounter it in mixed beech and silver fir woods, or even spruce woods, as long as they form a thick enough roof, since the Wood Warbler spends most of its time in the tree tops. In some parts of Europe it inhabits deciduous and mixed open woodland and in northern Germany it occurs in pine woods. It lives in lowland regions and hills and in the mountains up to an altitude of about 1,500 m. Soon after the birds have returned from their winter quarters and have found mates, the female looks for a suitable site for the nest and begins to build it.

The foundations of the nest, which is spherical when completed, are grass and leaves. The lining consists of softer material, such as moss, or occasionally feathers. The nest is less neat in appearance than that of other warblers and is usually not so well concealed. It is often situated in a hollow, in low grass, fallen leaves, heather, bilberry plants, etc. The nest is built in 2—3 days by the female, which receives moral support, but no actual assistance, from the male.

In May or June the female lays six or seven eggs at intervals of 1 day and generally starts to incubate them when the fourth one has been laid. The eggs are marked with rusty and dark brown surface spots and streaks on a white ground and often have ash-grey deep spots showing through the shell. Frequently the markings are concentrated at the blunt end of the egg. The Wood Warbler usually nests once, at most twice, a year. The eggs are incubated for 13—14 days, during which the female has to look for its food itself. After the young are hatched, the male does most of the feeding, but bit by bit leaves this work to the female. By the time the young are ready to leave the nest they are fed entirely by the female.

The Goldcrest
(Regulus regulus)

Dimensions of the eggs (in mm):
Mean — 13.6 × 10.3
Maxima — 14.8 × 11.1 and 14.7 × 11.3
Minima — 12.2 × 10 and 13.4 × 9.5

The Goldcrest is the smallest European bird and is also apparently the smallest songbird. It has a close affinity for coniferous trees and is therefore commonest in spruce and silver fir woods. It also nests in mixed growths if they contain at least a few groups of conifers. Both partners cooperate in the building of the nest, which starts at the end of March. Compared with the size of the bird, the nest is a huge, almost spherical structure ingeniously woven into horizontal silver fir and spruce branches. It has thick walls and narrows towards the relatively small opening at the top, evidently to prevent the eggs from falling out during high winds. The Goldcrest mainly uses moss, lichen, bast, cobwebs and cocoons in the construction of its nest and lines it with wool and feathers. The outer diameter is 9—11 cm and the inner diameter 6 cm. It is situated very high (8—12 m) above the ground and is so well concealed in the boughs that it is extremely hard to find. In very rare cases the Goldcrest may build somewhat lower, e.g. in a juniper bush. The nest may take 12 or more days to complete.

The first clutches can appear at the end of April, but they are usually produced at the beginning of May. A second clutch is laid in June. Each clutch contains eight to ten yellowish or white eggs covered with dark blotches, which at the blunt end are concentrated to form an indistinct ring. They are incubated for 12—17 days by the female. The male, however, helps to feed the young, which remain in the nest for 15—16 days (according to some sources up to 21 days). After leaving the nest the young are said to congregate near it for a further 18—37 days.

The Spotted Flycatcher
(*Muscicapa striata*)

Dimensions of the eggs (in mm):
Mean — *18.6×13.9*
Maxima — *21.2×14.3 and 19.6×15.1*
Minima — *17×14 and 18.3×12.9*

The Spotted Flycatcher inhabits airy deciduous, mixed and conifer woods. As a niche-nester, it primarily requires old, large trees, but is sometimes content with a forked branch. It is a frequent inhabitant of parks, large gardens, avenues and cemeteries and is found relatively high up in the mountains, sometimes right to the limit of the forest belt. Near human communities it nests under the roofs of summer-houses and sheds, in creepers on the walls of houses and in nesting boxes.

The untidy nest is usually situated 2—5 m above the ground, but seldom higher, and although it is built by both the mates, the female plays the major part. It is completed in 3—8 days and is made of moss, roots, blades of grass and leaves; the well is lined with wool and hair. It is 9—19 cm across and 4—6 cm high and the well is 5—6 cm across and 4-5 cm deep.

The Spotted Flycatcher starts to lay about 1 week after the nest is finished, in May or June. It nests once a year, but part of the population certainly nests twice. The clutch usually contains five (in extreme cases four to nine) greenish-grey or bluish-green eggs with mauvish-grey deep spots and vivid, rusty-brown surface spots. On occasion, the spots run into each other at the blunt end. The female sometimes starts to sit on the clutch when the second egg has been laid. It has not been reliably demonstrated whether the male also incubates the eggs, but it is more likely that only the female sits on them and that the male keeps it supplied with food. The incubation period is 12—13 days and the young are fed by the parents and remain in the nest for the same length of time.

The Dunnock
(Prunella modularis)

Dimensions of the eggs (in mm):
Mean — *19.2 × 14.4*
Maxima — *22.5 × 15 and 20.2 × 16*
Minima — *17.5 × 14 and 19.8 × 13.2*

In Western Europe, e.g. in Britain and France, the Dunnock inhabits parks, gardens and orchards, where it normally nests in shrubs and hedges. As we travel east, the situation alters and in Central Europe this secretive bird lives in coniferous forests at high altitudes. It is also found in mixed woods and fir forests in lowlands and hills. At the end of the last century it was still a mountain-dweller and its descent to low altitudes is a secondary phenomenon.

The Dunnock lives in cool, shady spots and keeps close to the ground, except for the male, which sometimes likes to sing from the top of a tree. The nest is hidden away among the densest twigs of young trees, preferably conifers. It is usually well concealed on all sides, but can easily be identified by its characteristic construction. It is made mainly of green moss and small twigs and the well is lined with fine blades of grass, hair, feathers and — and this is the characteristic feature — with the red spore cases of mosses. The nest is built by the female.

The Dunnock nests twice a year, at least at low altitudes, from the middle of April to July. The clutch contains four or five (in rare cases seven) deep bluish-green eggs. As we already know, it is not usual for birds which nest in the open to lay single-coloured eggs. Sometimes only the female incubates the eggs, while sometimes both the birds share in the task. The incubation period is 13—14 days. The parent birds both feed the young, which leave the nest at the age of about 2 weeks, but do not start to flutter about for several more days.

The Tree Pipit
(*Anthus trivialis*)

Dimensions of the eggs (in mm):
Mean   — 20.4 × 15.5
Maxima — 22.5 × 16.3 and 20.3 × 16.6
Minima — 18.3 × 15.2 and 20 × 13.2

The Tree Pipit nests in the open, lighter parts of all types of forests — at the periphery, in clearings and in glades — at all altitudes. For nesting it chooses a spot with low ground vegetation. The nest is situated on the ground, usually in a shallow hollow, where there is good cover.

It is a somewhat carelessly built structure made mainly of grass blades, fragments of leaves and plenty of moss. The smooth-walled well is often lined with hair, but may have no lining at all. The whole nest measures 9—13 cm across and the well 5—7 cm across, while the nest is 6—7 cm high and the well is 3.5—6 cm deep.

Some pairs of Tree Pipits nest once a year, others twice, from April to July. Few birds have such variable eggs. Looking at a large series of the Tree Pipit's eggs, it is difficult to believe that one species can produce such a variety of shapes and colours. In general, three main basic colours can be differentiated — red, brown and grey. In each of these groups the eggs can be further subdivided according to the shape and distribution of the spots. In one there are dense small spots and blotches, in another the spots are large and run into one another. The deep spots show up faintly against the dark ground colour, while the surface spots are either brownish-red or dark brown. Various types of streaks, as well as round spots, also occur. The female incubates the eggs for 12—14 days and is occasionally brought food by the male. The young are fed by both the parent birds and leave the nest after 12—14 days.

The Yellow Wagtail
(Motacilla flava)

Dimensions of the eggs (in mm):
Mean   — 18.7 × 13.9
Maxima   — 21 × 14.3 and 19.7 × 15.2
Minimum — 16.3 × 12.8

The Yellow Wagtail inhabits extensive lowland and wide valleys, where it is found mainly near water, in wet meadows, etc. It can also be seen in relatively dry meadows and fields, however. Scattered trees and bushes or tall plants are popular nesting sites. The male returns in the spring a little earlier than the female and chooses a nesting territory, where it keeps the female company while the latter builds the nest. The nest is a loosely woven structure made of stems and small roots and the well is lined with hair and wool and sometimes with feathers. It is generally situated in a hollow under a tuft of grass or a lump of soil, but sometimes in a cornfield, clover field or even a potato field. If there are eminences, hillocks, ridges or road and railway embankments in the area, the Yellow Wagtail likes to nest at their foot.

The eggs are laid in May or June. It is not yet known whether later clutches are substitute or normal second clutches. The nest contains four to six yellowish, brownish-green or reddish eggs so thickly speckled with greyish-brown spots that the ground colour may be almost invisible. Sometimes they are thinly marked with blackish-brown spots or filamentous tracings. They are incubated for 13—16 days by the female, which starts to brood when the last egg is laid. The young, which are fed by both the parent birds, leave the nest after 13 days, but are not capable of making short flights for another 4—5 days.

The Grey Wagtail
(Motacilla cinerea)

Dimensions of the eggs (in mm):
Mean   —   *19 × 14.4*
Maxima —   *21.7 × 14.3 and 24 × 16*
Minima —   *17 × 14.1 and 19 × 12.7*

The Grey Wagtail has a far stronger affinity for water than the Yellow Wagtail. Together with the Ring Ouzel it inhabits the banks of clear mountain and foothill streams in the middle of forests. In the mountains it actually follows the course of the streams high up into the alpine belt — in the Alps, for example, to an altitude of 2,700 m. In the lowlands it nests beside lakes and sluices, as well as near streams, canals and small rivers. It arrives in its nesting area in March.

The nest is a large structure and looks like a heap of dry vegetable material. It is built mainly of dry blades of grass, leaves, twigs and moss; the relatively small well is lined with hair, soft fibres and feathers. The nest is practically always situated near water — in holes in the bank, between the roots of trees standing by the water, in the masonry of old bridges, in conduits, near mill-races and in the stonework of dams and canals. Very occasionally it is found loosely placed in the twigs of young trees.

The nesting period extends into July, as the Grey Wagtail always nests twice, and sometimes three times, a year. The female lays four to six (generally five) eggs, which resemble those of the Yellow Wagtail, but are yellower and usually have reddish-brown spots. The female starts to brood when the last egg is laid. It is regularly relieved by the male, which plays the greater part in the nesting activities. The incubation period is 12—14 days. The young leave the nest after 12—13 days, but the family remains united for a long time.

The Starling
(Sturnus vulgaris)

Dimensions of the eggs (in mm):
Mean   —   *29.6 × 21.1*
Maxima —   *34.9 × 21 and 29.2 × 22.6*
Minima —   *26.3 × 20 and 27.1 × 19.4*

The Starling originally inhabited deciduous and mixed forests at low and high altitudes, where it still nests in tree hollows. It has spread to cultivated country, however, and has even become a camp-follower of man. In some regions the provision of nesting boxes is an ancient tradition and it was these which tempted the Starling to approach human habitations. The first reports of the Starling's nesting in nesting boxes date back to the sixteenth century, but it was not until the seventeenth century that it became a widespread custom. The Starling now nests on buildings and tiled roofs, in cracked walls and under rafters. In woods, avenues and parks it inhabits old woodpecker holes.

The male looks for a hole for the nest and is sometimes obliged to wage a fierce battle with birds which have already occupied it. It also lays the foundations of the nest, which is completed by the female. The foundations consist of coarse straw and blades of grass and sometimes include twigs, finer blades of grass and feathers. The material is fetched by the male. Sometimes we can find fresh flowers in the lining of the nest.

The female lays the first clutch at the end of April or the beginning of May. It usually contains five or six eggs, but sometimes eight or nine. A few older Starlings nest again in June. Young females lay fewer eggs. The eggs are light blue and unspotted. They are incubated during the night by the female and during the daytime by the male. The young, which are hatched in 14 days, are fed by both the parent birds. They grow rapidly, so that at 13 days they have attained their final weight and their feathers have started to grow. From then on the parents no longer feed them in the nest and in nesting boxes their hungry beaks can be seen protruding from the opening. When 18—21 days old they leave the nest. The parents feed them a few days longer and the young then gather together in flocks and hunt for food themselves.

The Greenfinch
(*Carduelis chloris*)

Dimensions of the eggs (in mm):
Mean   —   *20.4 × 14.7*
Maxima — *24.1 × 14.2 and 23 × 16.1*
Minima — *17.8 × 14.7 and 21.5 × 12.2*

The Greenfinch is a common bird in all types of country with an abundance of trees. It occurs in light deciduous and mixed woods and on the outskirts of coniferous forests. It is likewise not shy of man and is frequently seen in gardens, parks and human communities in general. It returns early in the spring and soon starts to nest, so that three clutches a year are no rarity. The first clutches appear at the end of March and the beginning of April, and as deciduous trees, at this time, have hardly started to bud, we find the first nests mainly in conifers, at a height of 2—6 m above the ground. Later on they can also be found in the tops of thick bushes and trees, often in the groove between the trunk and the shoot of a young branch. The female does most or all of the building. The nest is generally made of twigs, dry grass and small roots; the well is lined with horsehair, feathers, hair or fine roots. Each time the Greenfinch breeds, it usually builds a new nest. The first and second clutches contain five or six eggs, the third two to four. The eggs are whitish or bluish-white and are marked with indistinct reddish- and mauvish-grey deep spots and rusty-brown surface spots. The eggs are incubated for 12—14 days by the female, which is fed by the male during the whole of this period and also for a short time after the young are hatched. The young are afterwards fed by both parents. They leave the nest at 12—17 days, before they are fully fledged. Until they fly away, their bell-like voices can be heard as they perch near the nest.

The Goldfinch
(Carduelis carduelis)

Dimensions of the eggs (in mm):
Mean   — 17.1 × 12.9
Maxima — 19 × 13.5 and 18.5 × 13.7
Minima — 15.1 × 12 and 15.2 × 11.9

The Goldfinch lives in open country and avoids large forests. Its favourite haunts are the outskirts of villages and towns with numerous avenues and groups of trees. During the nesting season it also appears in airy deciduous and mixed woods, in fields and riverside woods and even relatively high up in the mountains, again near human communities. As a rule, the neat little nest is situated in a tree, fruit trees being particularly popular, but it may be built in tall bushes, in the fork of the terminal branches 2—10 m above the ground. The nest has thick walls and at the base it is generally made fast to the branch with fibres.

It is made of dry stems and small twigs, the walls are faced with moss and lichen and the well is lined with fine roots and various fibres, cocoon silk and fluff. The whole nest is 7—8 cm across and 5—6 cm high and the well is 5 cm across and 3 cm deep. The nest is built by the female.

The first clutches of four to six eggs appear at the end of April. The eggs are bluish-white or whitish and are marked with reddish-brown surface spots and sometimes with a few almost black spots. The deep spots are ash-grey. The Goldfinch generally nests twice a year and the eggs are incubated for 12—13 days by the female, which also keeps the young covered for the first few days. The young, which remain in the nest for 14 days, are fed by both parents, first of all with insects and then with seeds softened in the adult birds' crop.

The Linnet
(Acanthis cannabina)

Dimensions of the eggs (in mm):
Mean — 18.1 × 13.2
Maxima — 21.2 × 13.6 *and* 18.3 × 14.4
Minima — 16.3 × 12.8 *and* 19.3 × 11.9

The Linnet avoids high mountains and large woods with tall timber, but otherwise nests in parks and orchards and on the outskirts of woods. Its favourite places, however, are unfertile ground with thickets and stunted trees, small copses, warm hillsides overgrown with shrubs, sand dunes and hedges. It is likewise to be found in peat-bogs with small and stunted trees.

The Linnet generally nests not more than 2 m above the ground and distinctly prefers bushes and small trees to the tops of tall trees, although it is by no means unusual to find its nest in the latter. The nest is generally well hidden and we must part the branches to find it. It is a firm, though not very tidy, structure, whose inner layer consists ot twigs, roots, grass blades and fragments of bast. The smoothly turned well is lined with hairs, wool and feathers and sometimes with pieces of paper and material as well. Although the nest is built entirely by the female, it is completed in only about 4 days.

Clutches of four to six, but not more then eight, eggs appear in the nest from the middle of April until July (and sometimes until August). The eggs are whitish-blue and are speckled with small rusty red or blackish brown and purple spots, dots and squiggles. Almost unspotted eggs are likewise not rare. The eggs are incubated for 12—13 days, mainly by the female, which is relieved by the male for a short time during the afternoon. The young remain in the nest 12—14 days and are fed by both parents. The Linnet generally nests twice a year.

The Bullfinch
(Pyrrhula pyrrhula)

Dimensions of the eggs (in mm):
Mean — *22.2×15.1*
Maxima — *22.1×13.6 and 20.6×15.7*
Minima — *17.5×14.3 and 18×12.6*

The Bullfinch must be regarded as a forest-dwelling bird with a special affinity for coniferous trees, despite the fact that during the nesting season it is also to be found elsewhere. It prefers woods with undergrowth to old, tall timber and likes the edge of glades, clearings, tracks and paths. Mixed and coniferous forests at moderate and high altitudes are its main abode, but given favourable conditions it also lives in low-lying country. It likewise nests in old, rambling gardens and parks.

The nest is generally situated in a conifer, as a rule beside or close to the trunk, at a height of up to 2 m above the ground. The Bullfinch does not avoid deciduous trees and bushes altogether, however. The base of the nest is made of dry twigs, small roots, upper rootlets, moss, leaves and lichen and the well is lined with plant and animal fluff.

Compared with other finches, the Bullfinch is a late nester. It nests twice a year, starting in May or June. The eggs are pale blue with large, blotchy, reddish-grey deep spots and with rusty or violet-brown surface spots, which are usually at the blunt end. Here and there the spots are interspersed with black dots and squiggles. The four or five (sometimes six) eggs are incubated by the female, which starts to brood before laying the last egg and does not leave them until they are hatched. The incubation period is 13—14 days. In a few cases the male has been known to relieve the female for a short time. If the female sits on the eggs, the male feeds it from time to time from its crop. The young remain in the nest for 16—18 days.

The Chaffinch
(Fringilla coelebs)

Dimensions of the eggs (in mm):
Mean — 19.3 × 14.7
Maxima — 22.9 × 14.5 and 19.8 × 15.7
Minima — 17.1 × 13.7 and 19.5 × 13

The Chaffinch is one of the most familiar of our native birds. Wherever there are trees, there are Chaffinches, in parks and gardens as well as in the woods, and in the lowlands as well as in the mountains. In the spring we can see the singing males right on the edge of the forest belt, where the tall timber borders on the stunted pine belt. We can easily identify the Chaffinch's nest, which is a firmly woven structure made chiefly of moss and lichen, together with blades of grass. Birch bark, cocoon silk and pieces of paper are sometimes added. The well is softly lined with hair, feathers, wool, etc.

The female builds the nest so early that it is generally finished before the trees start to burgeon. It is very rare for the male to lend a hand. The nest may be situated in a fork in a horizontal or sloping branch, or in the groove between a branch and the trunk, at varying heights. Its outer diameter is 8.5—10.5 cm, its height 6.5—8 cm and the well is 5 cm across and 4.5—5 cm deep.

Between the middle of April and July, the female lays two clutches comprising five or six (in exceptional cases up to eight) eggs of variable colouring. The eggs may be light brown, reddish-grey, greyish-blue or light blue and are marked with reddish-brown blotches and blackish-brown speckles, or with large, blackish-brown spots with blurred contours. The indistinct deep spots are mauvish-grey. The eggs are incubated by the female, which is sometimes relieved by the male. The female hunts for food itself while brooding, but is also brought food by the male. The young are hatched in 12—13 days and remain for 13—14 days in the nest. Again, the female is largely responsible for feeding them. Chaffinches often use the same nest twice in succession.

The Corn Bunting
(Emberiza calandra)

Dimensions of the eggs (in mm):
Mean — *24.1 × 17.2*
Maxima — *28.6 × 18 and 26.2 × 19.5*
Minima — *19 × 17.8 and 26.4 × 15.5*

This large bunting inhabits stretches of lowland with scattered trees and bushes. It seems to have a special predilection for wet meadows and clover or lucerne fields in river basins. The female usually makes the nest in a small hollow in the ground — in a meadow, among clover or lucerne, on a boundary ridge or in a ditch — and sometimes in shrubs or tall weeds, up to 30 cm above the ground. The building materials are blades of grass, leaves and roots and the nest is lined with wool, soft parts of plants, fur, horsehair and isolated feathers.

The Corn Bunting nests twice a year, between the end of April and July. The clutch usually contains four or five (rarely three to seven) greyish-red, greyish-white or dingy flesh-coloured eggs with reddish-grey deep spots and blackish-brown surface spots and speckles. Filamentous and vermiform markings are also characteristic for the eggs of this bunting. The spots are often concentrated round the blunt end of the egg, so that the rest is practically unmarked.

The female begins to brood before the clutch is complete and receives neither assistance nor food from the male. The incubation period is 12—14 days. About once an hour the bird leaves the eggs and flies in search of food. The young, which are fed almost entirely by the female, remain in the nest for about 9—12 days and then disperse round it. Non-participation by the male in the building of the nest, the incubation of the eggs (apart from a few exceptions) and the feeding of the young is evidently associated with polygamy. The extent of this phenomenon among Corn Buntings, i.e. whether it is individual or general, has not yet been determined, however.

The Yellowhammer
(*Emberiza citrinella*)

Dimensions of the eggs (in mm):
Mean   —   21.6 × 16.3
Maxima —   25.9 × 15 and 23.3 × 17.5
Minima —   18.9 × 15.3 and 19.5 × 15

The Yellowhammer is an unassuming bird noted particularly for its characteristic song. It nests in any type of country where it finds shrubs and small groups of trees. It is also common on the outskirts of human communities, but is absent in compact, deep forests. Following clearings and river valleys, it ascends high up into the mountains.

The nest is built on or close to the ground and is made by the female. Its base is woven together from dry stems, small twigs and leaves. This is surmounted by a layer of finer stems and blades of grass, sometimes together with moss, and the well is lined with the finest vegetable materials and with fur or horsehair. The nest is 8.8—13 cm across and 5.5—8 cm high, while the well is 5—8 cm across and 4—5.5 cm deep. Nests above the ground are generally larger than ground nests.

As a rule, there are two clutches a year, but three clutches are not unknown. They are laid between April and July and usually contain four to six eggs, again of very variable colouring. The eggs may be white with a grey, red or blue tinge and have ash-grey deep spots and large numbers of surface spots and speckles. They also have typical filamentous and vermiform markings twisted into various shapes. The female begins to brood after laying the last egg and is seldom relieved by the male. The incubation period is 11—14 days. The young remain in the nest for the same length of time and are fed by both the parent birds, first of all with softened food from their crop and later directly, from beak to beak. The family remains intact for about 10 days after the young have left the nest.

The Reed Bunting
(Emberiza schoeniclus)

Dimensions of the eggs (in mm):
Mean — *19.7 × 14.7*
Maxima — *22.1 × 14.5 and 20.5 × 16*
Minimum — *17.4 × 13.5*

The Reed Bunting often keeps company with Reed Warblers, as it has the same type of habitat — wet ground, swamps and belts of swamp plants near water. It is very fond of the intermediate zone between the dry ground and the rush or osier belt, i.e. strips of sedge and reed-grass, especially if it contains scattered willows and other bushes.

The nest, which is built on or close to the ground, is well hidden in thick grass, reed-grass, rushes, etc. Sometimes it is situated in a low bush. Normally it is placed on a clump of tangled plants or is wedged between stems. It is built by the female and is a relatively loose structure made of plant stems and leaves, moss and peat and is lined with hair, wool and other soft material. Many nests are quite plain and have no lining.

Between April and July a couple of Reed Buntings rear two, and occasionally three, generations of young. The clutch contains four to six eggs, which are relatively dark compared with those of other buntings. The ground colour is light brown or greyish-yellow and the markings consist of ash-grey deep spots and typical brownish-red or brownish-black surface spots, speckles and vermiform and filamentous tracings. The eggs are hatched by the female, which is sometimes relieved by the male. The young are hatched in 12—14 days and remain in the nest 11—13 days. After leaving the nest they hide in the surrounding vegetation and are still fed for a time by the parents.

The House Sparrow
(Passer domesticus)

Dimensions of the eggs (in mm):
Mean — 22.5 × 15.7
Maxima — 25.3 × 15 and 22.4 × 16.6
Minima — 19.4 × 15.6 and 20.8 × 13.9

The House Sparrow is a constant companion of man. It is widely distributed in all human communities, from isolated cottages and villages to great cities.

The nest is built in the most diverse sites — under roofs, behind gutter-pipes, on facades, in nesting boxes, in the nests of House Martins and the burrows of Sand Martins, in short, in every conceivable hole or niche. Here it is an untidy heap of straw, stems, cotton wool, rags and feathers. Otherwise sparrows nest in trees, where they build a large spherical nest, with a side entrance, in the branches, usually at a safe distance above the ground. Sometimes we can see a collection of dozens of sparrows' nests in a single tree, rather on the lines of the colonies of weavers, to which sparrows are related. The nest is built by both partners.

The House Sparrow normally nests two or three times a year and sometimes even four times. It is therefore not surprising that it often multiplies to an impossible degree. One clutch usually contains five or six eggs (maximum ten). The nesting season may start at the beginning of April, but generally in the middle, and ends in July or August. The whitish, greenish or bluish eggs are frequently marked with sparsely distributed, clear or blurred, grey or brown spots, while at times the spots are small, but very thick. They are often denser at the blunt end of the egg. The male and the female incubate the eggs for 13—14 days and the young leave the nest at the age of 15 days. They are fed by both parents, first of all with crushed insects from their crop and later with whole insects from their beak.

The Tree Sparrow
(Passer montanus)

Dimensions of the eggs (in mm):
Mean — *19.2 × 14.2*
Maxima — *22.6 × 13.7 and 19.3 × 15.4*
Minima — *16.4 × 13.2 and 17.5 × 13*

Unlike the House Sparrow, the Tree Sparrow is rarely seen in towns and large villages, but is a common sight in old orchards, parks and lanes and on the outskirts of villages and woods. It usually nests in tree holes, but also in openings and holes in walls, in rock fissures, in holes in the walls of clay-pits, in Sand Martin burrows, in the framework of wells, in the nests of large birds and in hay-stacks. It also likes to nest in nesting boxes intended and prepared for other birds. The nest is an untidy structure made of straw, twigs, hairs and different fibres and lined with feathers. Like the House Sparrow, the Tree Sparrow also sleeps in nests when not actually nesting.

The Tree Sparrow can breed up to three times a year, from the middle of April until August. The clutches contain four to six (maximum ten) very variably coloured eggs. The ground colour is usually white, less frequently green, and the markings consist of thickly distributed brown and grey spots which sometimes run together to form marbling. Incubation, which lasts 13—14 days, starts when the last egg is laid. Both the parents take turns to sit on the eggs. The young leave the nest at the age of 14—15 days. As soon as they attain independence and are no longer fed by the adult birds, they join together in large flocks and fly out into the fields in search of food. They eat a greater proportion of insects than the House Sparrow.

INDEX OF COMMON NAMES

INDEX OF LATIN NAMES